Little Caesar

Wisconsin/Warner Bros. Screenplay Series

Little Caesar

Edited with an introduction by

Gerald Peary

Published for the Wisconsin Center for Film and Theater Research by
The University of Wisconsin Press

Published 1981

The University of Wisconsin Press
114 North Murray Street
Madison, Wisconsin 53715

The University of Wisconsin Press, Ltd.
1 Gower Street
London WC1E 6HA, England

First printing

Printed in the United States of America

For LC CIP information see the colophon

ISBN 0-299-08450-7 cloth; 0-299-08454-X paper

Publication of this volume has been assisted by a grant from
The Brittingham Fund, Inc.

Contents

Foreword

In donating the Warner Film Library to the Wisconsin Center for Film and Theater Research in 1969, along with the RKO and Monogram film libraries and UA corporate records, United Artists created a truly great resource for the study of American film. Acquired by United Artists in 1957, during a period when the major studios sold off their films for use on television, the Warner library is by far the richest portion of the gift, containing eight hundred sound features, fifteen hundred short subjects, nineteen thousand still negatives, legal files, and press books, in addition to screenplays for the bulk of the Warner Brothers product from 1930 to 1950. For the purposes of this project, the company has granted the Center whatever publication rights it holds to the Warner films. In so doing, UA has provided the Center another opportunity to advance the cause of film scholarship.

Our goal in publishing these Warner Brothers screenplays is to explicate the art of screenwriting during the thirties and forties, the so-called Golden Age of Hollywood. In preparing a critical introduction and annotating the screenplay, the editor of each volume is asked to cover such topics as the development of the screenplay from its source to the final shooting script, differences between the final shooting script and the release print, production information, exploitation and critical reception of the film, its historical importance, its directorial style, and its position within the genre. He is also encouraged to go beyond these guidelines to incorporate supplemental information concerning the studio system of motion picture production.

We could set such an ambitious goal because of the richness of the script files in the Warner Film Library. For many film titles, the files might contain the property (novel, play, short story, or original story idea), research materials, variant drafts of scripts (from story outline to treatment to shooting script), post-production items such as press books and dialogue continuities, and legal records (details of the acquisition of the property, copyright registration, and contracts with actors and directors). Editors of the Wisconsin/Warner Bros. Screenplay Series receive copies of all the materials, along with prints of the films (the most authoritative ones available for reference purposes), to use in preparing the introductions and annotating the final shooting scripts.

In the process of preparing the screenplays for publication, typographical errors were corrected, punctuation and capitalization were modernized, and the format was redesigned to facilitate readability.

Unless otherwise specified, the photographs are frame enlargements taken from a 35-mm print of the film provided by United Artists.

In 1977 Warner Brothers donated the company's production records and distribution records to the University of Southern California and Princeton University, respectively. These materials are now available to researchers and complement the contents of the Warner Film Library donated to the Center by United Artists.

Tino Balio
General Editor

Introduction

Little Caesar Takes over the Screen

Gerald Peary

Without the advent of Prohibition, the saga of *Little Caesar* could not have existed. By the mid-1920s, organized crime had taken sufficient advantage of the Eighteenth Amendment, law since January 1920, to establish a bootlegging empire across America, and Al Capone had taken control in Chicago. Judge John Lyle, Capone's eventual prosecutor, wrote, "We might arbitrarily take the year 1926 as the dawn of the Great Awakening."[1] Suddenly the media were saturated with tabloid exposés of racketeering, these detailing the structure of the urban underworld, decrying the failure of Prohibition, and noting the collusion among mobsters, politicians, and crooked law enforcers. The "hard-boiled" detective story emerged in the pages of Joseph Shaw's *Black Mask* magazine, written by Dashiell Hammett and others. The George Abbott–Philip Dunning musical *Broadway*, in which tough-talking, modern-day racketeers stalked the stage between the songs and the banter, opened in September 1926 in New York and played for seventy-three weeks.

Broadway was sold to Hollywood for the record price of $250,000, though Universal Pictures postponed production until 1929, when sound was perfected for the musical numbers. *Broadway*'s phenomenal stage success spawned an immediate major cycle of gangster films in 1927 and 1928. *Chicago after Mid-*

1. John H. Lyle, *The Dry and Lawless Years* (Englewood Cliffs, N.J.: Prentice-Hall, 1960), p. 188.

night (FBO) and *The Heart of Broadway* (Rayart) stole their plots from the hoofer melodramatics of *Broadway*. More original—and also more violent—were Josef von Sternberg's *Underworld* and *The Racket* (both Paramount) and *Dressed to Kill* (Fox).

As bloodshed increased on the screen and as mobsters were vividly portrayed, even glamourized, censorship boards across the country took offense. In 1928, Chicago city officials turned a vigilant eye upon *Dressed to Kill*, about a modishly attired gang of murderers, and pulled the film from the Loop's Monroe theater. In New York, all references to Tammany Hall and to dishonest politicians were deleted from Raoul Walsh's *Me Gangster* (Fox), an alleged true-life autobiography of a criminal. From *The Racket*, close-ups of the gangster's gun and of mobsters shooting a policeman were cut out, as well as scenes impugning the integrity of law officials. "Women's clubs and mother's clubs throughout the land are protesting the output of underworld pictures," *The New Yorker* reported in October 1928, and such films disappeared from Hollywood production schedules.

The new conservatism was less reflective of a drastic law-and-order shift of the nation in 1928 than of the gradual souring of millions of persons toward the "open city" of the Jazz Age twenties, with its flaming youth, fast cars, myriad Prohibition violations, and alarming crime rate. As Herbert Hoover, newly elected Republican president, stated in his inaugural address of March 4, 1929, "The strong man must at all times be alert to the attack of insidious disease. The most malign of all these dangers is disregard and disobedience of law."

As if on cue, a cycle of "law-and-order" movies, which dramatized the struggle against the underworld from the police vantage, was ushered into America's theaters. Paramount Pictures used its press sheet publicity for *Woman Trap*, a typical 1929 police film, to advise theater managers to "invite the police force to be your guests the opening day." If this wasn't enough, George Bancroft, the prototype gangster of silent film because of "Bull" Weed in *Underworld*, played a policeman in *The Dragnet* and a gangster-turned-police-chief in *The Mighty* (both Paramount). These transformations were as startling and unexpected as James Cagney's conversion from the rackets to the FBI in *G Men* in 1935.

During this time, *Little Caesar* was conceived by W. R. Burnett, who researched and wrote his novel in Chicago in the winter of 1928. It was published by Dial Press in June 1929 and purchased by Warner Brothers on March 7, 1930, for immediate production. But between these last two events, American life turned upside down. The stock market crashed, and the country slipped quickly into the Great Depression. Bread lines grew long in the winter of 1929–30. The unemployed demonstrated in Seattle, Los Angeles, and Chicago in February 1930. In March, Milwaukee opened a municipal kitchen. And President Hoover's census in April 1930 uncovered severe job loss throughout the land: "2,429,000 were looking for work, and 755,000 had been laid off the job. Thus, the unemployed totaled 3,184,000."[2] Still, the federal government kept denying a depression. In September 1930, Assistant Secretary of State Julius Klein asserted that "we are climbing—soberly, unspectacularly—up to a healthier, normal situation."[3]

How was Hollywood reacting to the darkening economic conditions? Quite atypically, the film industry participated in the debate over the financial and spiritual health of the country. Whereas most pictures continued to be escapist and nontopical, studios used the gangster film genre in particular to reflect the discontent and alienation, the deep anxiety and hostility, of many Americans facing the Depression.

In some 1930 films, the gangster character became the scapegoat for the country's economic troubles. He was merged with the ruthless businessman whose shady speculative practices were blamed for precipitating the 1929 crash. William Powell played Natural Davis in *Street of Chance* (Paramount) as a Wall Street bonds broker by day and an Arnold Rothstein-type illegal gambler by night. The villain, Joe Palmer, of *Sweet Mama* (Warners) was a bank robber and murderer who hid behind the desk

2. Edward Robb Ellis, *A Nation in Torment* (New York: Coward-McCann, 1970), p. 121.

3. "When Do We Come out of It?" *American Magazine*, September 1930, p. 11.

of a legitimate business. According to instructions in the Warners script, Palmer's office should possess "a marked resemblance to a bank president's . . . or a high-powered financial executive."[4]

In a more significant group of 1930 films, the gangster was an ambitious underling, instead of the businessman boss, and thus much closer in class identification to the mass audience. In *Mothers Cry* and *Sinner's Holiday* (both Warners), the protagonists tried, through crime, to make as much money and achieve as much power as humanly possible. Both characters failed, barred from their employment and separated from family and loved ones, typical fates in the Depression. They were cheated for following the dominant oratory of the pre-crash era, when business and government lectured Americans to push hard on the job and inevitably reach the top. John Ford's little-known *Born Reckless* (Fox) was even more gloomy. Its protagonist tried to quit racketeering and go straight but he could find no employment. Wandering aimlessly in the belly of the city, he became an apt audience surrogate at a time of failing economy, when honesty promised no better fate than dishonesty.

If the little person was losing his way in 1930, what of Al Capone? He was experiencing business and personal problems that were exaggerated versions of the country's ills. Survivors of the Bugsy Moran gang organized against Capone to avenge the St. Valentine's Day Massacre of 1928, and the federal government pursued him for income-tax evasion. "I haven't had peace of mind in years," Capone confided to the press, between his appointments in federal court. "I have a wife and a beautiful home in Florida. If I could go there and forget it all, I'd be the happiest man in the world."[5]

Several months before the film *Little Caesar*, Warners released the first picture to utilize the faltering Capone as symbol of the Depression. The film was *The Doorway to Hell*, starring Lew

4. Earl Baldwin, "Sweet Mama," January 30, 1930, p. 43. Final screenplay, Warner Library, Wisconsin Center for Film and Theater Research, Madison, Wisconsin.

5. John Kobler, *Capone: The Life and World of Al Capone* (New York: Putnam, 1971), p. 247.

Ayres as Louis Ricarno, king of the Chicago rackets, who is expelled from his leadership and murdered by a rival gang. The film alluded to Capone's career in many concrete ways, from reenacting Capone's mediator role at a convention of organized crime in Atlantic City, 1929, to moving Ricarno's domicile to Florida.

Barely recalled today, *The Doorway to Hell* was an enormous success in November 1930, at the time of *Little Caesar*'s filming. Surely *Doorway*'s roman à clef strategy influenced the final form of *Little Caesar*. According to his autobiography, Jack Warner bought Burnett's novel because he thought the protagonist, Rico, "was a thinly disguised portrait of Al Capone."[6] Indeed, *Little Caesar* emerged as one of the few movies in which the film makers strove to come closer to real life than had their source. The Depression was not forgotten. As Mervyn LeRoy recalled in his autobiography, he wanted *Little Caesar*'s realism to reflect "that era of gloom and desperation that was the world of 1930."[7]

The Writing: Novel and Scripts

During his long and prolific career, W. R. Burnett wrote *High Sierra* (1940), *The Asphalt Jungle* (1949), and other crime classics. *Little Caesar*, his first novel, was conceived after Burnett came across a volume of sociology from the University of Chicago Press about the rise and fall of a certain Sam Cardinelli gang. "This account," wrote Burnett, "served as the nucleus for the novel that was originally called *The Furies*."[8] The working title, far too literary, was replaced by another, in a moment reminiscent of that night of creation in Mary Shelley's *Frankenstein*: "Rico, the leading figure, began to take on nightmare proportions. . . . I was afraid I was giving birth to a monster. But then a consoling thought came to me. . . . My leading figure, Rico

6. Jack L. Warner, with Dean Jennings, *My First Hundred Years in Hollywood* (New York: Random House, 1964), p. 199.

7. Mervyn LeRoy, as told to Dick Kleiner, *Mervyn LeRoy: Take One* (New York: Hawthorn, 1974), p. 94. Hereafter, page numbers in parentheses refer to *Mervyn LeRoy: Take One*.

8. W. R. Burnett, *Little Caesar*, 2d ed. (New York: Dial, 1958), p. 18.

Bandello, . . . was no monster at all, but merely a little Napoleon, a little Caesar."[9]

In his autobiography, Jack Warner bragged that "*Little Caesar* was one of the few novels I read from cover to cover as a potential picture property," having learned of it from songwriter Butch Davis in a Santa Fe railroad station in 1929. Davis lent the book to Warner, who read it during an all-night ride to San Diego. There he walked into a Western Union office and wired his story department in New York to buy the book.[10]

Not surprisingly, *Little Caesar*'s director offered an antithetical version of these events in *Mervyn LeRoy: Take One*. "One hot summer day in 1930," Warner presented him with galley proofs of a new book. "'I've got too much to do to read it tonight,'" Warner said. "'You read it and tell me what you think'" (p. 93). In this way, LeRoy discovered *Little Caesar*. "I read it straight through the night, my excitement heightening with every page. I didn't even go to sleep." He marched into Warner's office the next day and said, "This is what I've been looking for, Jack. This guy Burnett must have written this for me to do" (p. 93). Warner, however, did not share LeRoy's enthusiasm and was hesitant about buying such a hard-boiled book. Yet, after an hour of pleading, Warner agreed to the purchase and assigned LeRoy to direct.

Neither memory is to be trusted. *Little Caesar* was purchased from the Dial Press on March 7, 1930, *between* the two days mentioned in the Warner and LeRoy stories. Warner Brothers bought all rights to the novel for $15,000 and assigned two contract writers, Robert N. Lee and Francis Edwards Faragoh, to do a shooting script. Lee produced a seventy-five-page screen treatment, which he transformed into a temporary script dated April 30, 1930. Faragoh composed the final script of July 7, 1930, based on Lee's adaptation. The credit on the film version of *Little Caesar*, released in January 1931, reads "Continuity by Robert N. Lee, Screen Version and Dialogue by Francis Edwards Faragoh."

9. Burnett, *Little Caesar*, p. 22.
10. Warner, *My First Hundred Years in Hollywood*, pp. 199–200.

Lee was a logical choice to adapt *Little Caesar*. Although Ben Hecht's original story for *Underworld* is what film history recalls, Lee is the person actually credited on screen for writing Josef von Sternberg's acclaimed picture. He was also responsible for the original story for *The Mighty*, the 1929 gangster film starring *Underworld*'s George Bancroft. Lee's adeptness with crime material is evident in films he later composed at Warners: *The Big Shakedown* (1933), *From Headquarters* (1933), *Fog over Frisco* (1934), and *The Dragon Murder Case* (1934). His best script is *The Kennel Murder Case* (1933), from the S. S. Van Dine mystery novel, in which smooth direction by Michael Curtiz brought William Powell's Philo Vance a step away from Nick Charles and *The Thin Man* (1934).

If Lee was the consummate genre craftsman, snug in the studio, Francis Edwards Faragoh was the intellectual-in-Hollywood. He was drama editor of *Pearson's Magazine* and a founder-director of the New Playwrights Theatre. In 1927 he wrote *Pinwheel*, an expressionist drama performed at New York's Neighborhood Playhouse. J. Brooks Atkinson praised the production in the *New York Times* (February 4, 1927), saying that "perhaps for the first time in the city, the 'constructivist' stage setting . . . has been made serviceable."

It is hard to determine when Faragoh ventured to Hollywood, but in early 1930 he adapted *Back Pay* for Warners from a Fannie Hurst story. With this single credit, Faragoh was charged with the final script of *Little Caesar*. In 1931, Faragoh wrote two more screenplays at Warners: *Right of Way*, a melodrama set in the Canadian wilds, and *Too Young to Marry*, a *Babbitt*-like farce situated in a drab western town, directed by *Little Caesar*'s Mervyn LeRoy. Faragoh's more distinguished screen work came later: his 1935 adaptation of David Belasco's *Return of Peter Grimm* as an RKO vehicle for Lionel Barrymore, followed immediately by *Becky Sharp*, based on American playwright Langdon Mitchell's dramatization of Thackeray. The latter was a production of high quality, in early Technicolor, with settings by visionary stage designer Robert Edmond Jones and direction by Rouben Mamoulian. *Becky Sharp*'s design was matched by Faragoh's clever and idiosyncratic script, including a refreshingly amoral ending.

Honoring Jack Warner's interpretation of Rico Bandello as Al Capone, Lee constructed a temporary screenplay that retained elements from the novel that made the character resemble Capone: the proletariat Italian origins; the novice profession as a rabidly ambitious gunman; the fastidious dress and narcissism; the black locks, the jewelry, the spats. Lee transformed Burnett's Big Boy, who resembled the undereducated Capone within the novel, into a refined and polished boss. In that way, Rico would be the sole Capone figure of the film.

Lee's screenplay was more topical than the Burnett novel. Lee modeled Diamond Pete Montana after Diamond Jim Colosimo, boss of Chicago when Capone arrived there from New York. He based Rico's shooting of the new crime commissioner, McClure, on the infamous unsolved murder in 1926 of William McSwiggin, assistant state's attorney of Cook County.

The first two scenes in the movie of *Little Caesar* originate with Lee. Burnett's novel begins with Rico and Joe already entrenched in Sam Vettori's gang. Lee's script opens with a long shot of a gas station and the sound of gunfire, then cuts to Rico turning back the clock (see figure 1) to establish an alibi in an all-night diner, and concludes with the interrogation of Rico and Joe by the police. Lee invented the sequence in which Joe is hired as a dancer by DeVoss (see figure 4). And much of the last third of Lee's temporary script is intact in the film: Otero and Rico flee the police, Otero is shot in the alley, Rico hides in Ma Magdalena's fruit store. Finally, Lee conceived the symbolic images of the final scene (see figure 25): "With shoulders hunched against the wind, Rico is walking along a street in an industrial district. He pays no attention to a huge illuminated billboard which he is passing. In great letters the 24-sheet stand proclaims: The Laughing Singing Dancing Success. Olga Stassoff and Joe Massara in *Tipsy Topsy Turvy*.

Faragoh's script is notably more linear than Lee's version, with Rico's rise to the top plotted step by step. It is in Faragoh's script only that Rico serves an apprenticeship as bodyguard (figure 5), then threatens Vettori's leadership (figure 6), and finally assumes authority over the gang after the Bronze Peacock robbery. Earlier, Faragoh extended the sequence in the diner so that

Rico, much like a Shakespearean villain, may expound about his ambitions (figure 2). Faragoh invented the scene in which Rico "sells" himself to Sam Vettori. Afterward, Vettori introduces Rico to the gang and suddenly arrives at a nickname for his hireling—"Little Caesar, huh?" (figure 3).

Even more consequential, Faragoh added these five major scenes for the film:

1. Tony's funeral, which begins with long shots in homage to the 1924 processional for gangster Dion O'Banion (figure 14) and ends with black comedy, as the gang pretends to be in deep mourning for the person whom they have killed;

2. Rico's testimonial dinner, which Lee had relegated to descriptive words in a newspaper insert. Faragoh dramatized the banquet, basing the scene on the one in Burnett's novel (figures 15 and 16);

3. Rico's dressing up for the Big Boy before the admiring eyes of Otero (figure 18);

4. Rico's drinking in the flophouse (figure 23); and

5. Rico's being shot down and dying with the famous line, "Mother of Mercy, is this the end of Rico?" In Burnett's novel, the line begins, "Mother of God."

The Meaning of *Little Caesar*

As noted, Warner Brothers' earlier *Doorway to Hell* utilized Capone's life story as emblematic of the Depression era. The Capone-like protagonist, Louis Ricarno, had grown up an orphan in poverty, his little brother is murdered ruthlessly, and his wife deserts him for another. Deposed as Chicago gangleader, Ricarno is assassinated while living alone, and lonely, in a tawdry hotel room on the wrong side of the tracks. *Little Caesar* continues this dramatization of personal isolation and tragedy caused by the Depression and makes the proof even bleaker. If Louis Ricarno loses his family, Rico Bandello never mentions family at all. Nor does bachelor Rico have any love interests. Although Rico of the novel was given to "short bursts of lust" and quick affairs with molls, Rico of Lee's screenplay has no heterosexual concerns. In Burnett, Rico attended his testimonial banquet with Blondy Belle, the ex-girlfriend of Little Arnie Lorch. In Faragoh's scene, a "stag" Rico comments, "I'm glad you guys brought your molls with you." At the banquet in the movie, Rico is conspicuously flanked by two men.

What is the meaning of Rico without a female lover? A simple Freudian reading makes Rico a repressed homosexual, probably in love with Joe. But this interpretation, however evocative, seems inadequate to explain his familial isolation also. Lacking any loved ones, Rico is best understood as a symbol of the Depression, a person completely dislocated, solitary, forlorn.

In the novel, Rico arrives in Chicago from Youngstown, Ohio. In the film, Rico has no past home, only the dim knowledge that he comes from elsewhere than the big city. Therefore, when he finds that his criminal career has ebbed, he cannot even attempt to return to his "roots." He is condemned to wander the subterranean city until he meets his doom. In a scene invented for the movie by Faragoh, Rico lies about a fifteen-cents-a-night flophouse, a disheveled, alcoholic, and unemployed tramp. Thus a blatant 1930 Depression situation and setting are fused onto the gangster story.

Rico is alone, alone. Where is the traditional immigrant mother, who represents some semblance of moral order in the gangster's otherwise murky, chaotic life? Tom Powers in *The Public Enemy* (1931) has a kind mother who cares for him, as does Tony Camonte in *Scarface* (1932). But the only mother in *Little Caesar*, novel and film, is Tony's, not Rico's. Hardly noticed is a great irony, that Rico is rewarded with a surrogate, nightmare version of maternity. This is the filthy, witchlike hag "Ma" Magdalena, who shelters Rico from the police—for a price. She is a "fence"—greedy, untrustworthy. Different from the madonnalike mothers of other gangster movies, Ma thrives in the shyster, dog-eat-dog environment where everyone scrapes for a living. "Ma" waits until she has $150 in hand before she will hide Rico behind her fruit store, through a labyrinth of walkways into a secret room.

Mervyn LeRoy's movie set is based on this description from Burnett's novel: "She led him through a dark tunnel and back into the hide-out. A small, round opening just large enough to admit one person had been pierced in the wall." The symbolism is evident: this is Rico's flight back to the womb, albeit a surrogate one, before being thrust back onto the streets.

Rico's familial dissociation in the movie of *Little Caesar* is partly inspired by the publicized domestic turmoils of Capone. The film extends the Capone legend in another metaphoric way: for its lesson in American enterprise. The auspicious, step-by-step rise of Rico Bandello proves the most dynamic point of Capone's life: that crime can pay, and handsomely, at least for a time. A young thug such as Rico, with the right temperament and plenty of drive, can rise high, much like a young businessman with the right blend of personality credentials.

How does Rico differ from previous film gangsters who began low in the criminal organization? In almost all other pictures (except *Me, Gangster*), the gangster's rise to the top was briefly shown, if at all. James Cagney in *Sinner's Holiday* was the first to murder his boss. But Rico is the first to step *on* his bosses—Vettori, Arnie Lorch, Diamond Pete Montana—and over them, until only Big Boy keeps him from ruling the underworld. One writer has theorized that "the illicitness of [Rico's] incontrovertible power corresponds to the illicitness of the employee who would like to tell his boss to go to hell."[11]

For Mervyn LeRoy, Rico's obsessive drive to get higher and higher was his dominant theme for the movie: "Rico . . . was a man with a driving ambition to be on top. . . . He always tried to copy the man higher up, in hopes that he would thus assume the characteristics and eventually the job of that man" (p. 98). *Little Caesar* concentrates on carefully plotting Rico's advancement, dwelling on his acquisition of fine clothes and a fancy suite of rooms. His fall is only in the last minutes, a total reversal of fortune, a shock to Rico and maybe to viewers as well. *Time* (January 19, 1931) described these final moments: "His luck changes. He loses his power, his money, becomes a flophouse derelict, and finally dies behind a billboard, chewed by bullets from a policeman's machine-gun."

11. Parker Tyler, *The Hollywood Hallucination* (New York: Simon & Schuster, 1944), p. 114.

What went wrong? Certainly there was no precedent in the Horatio Alger story, which held only the prospect for even greater success for a hero who has followed the rules of conduct appropriate to his milieu. "Ragged Dick," for instance, finishes as "Richard Hunter, Esq. . . . a young gentleman on the way to fame and fortune."

Why did the real-life gangster Al Capone fall? Many have theorized that he was too devoted to the limelight. He was the last major figure of organized crime to seek celebrity and he probably paid for insisting that the world know his name. Said social historian Andrew Sinclair: "His successors are harder fish to net. They have heeded Brecht's rhetorical question, 'What is robbing a bank compared with founding a bank?' And they have been rewarded with both the millions and the ease and the semirespectability that Alphonse Capone wanted all his life and never found."[12]

Rico Bandello likewise was finished because he *had* to respond to the insults to his name, planted in the newspaper by Flaherty the policeman. Defending his wilted honor, a ragged and derelict Rico returns to the open, where he is shot and killed. As he dies, his magnificent creation dies with him. "Mother of Mercy, is this the end of Rico?" His name is his last word.

What does death mean for Rico? In gangster movies of the twenties—*Underworld*, for example—a gang leader who committed terrible deeds, including murder, was allowed to absolve himself gracefully of his sins through heroic sacrifice, often to save the sacred love of a young and innocent couple. By giving up his life for this moral cause, he would instantly bring meaning to his existence, demonstrating knowledge of his sins and a desire for reformation. As Parker Tyler says of the prototype crime story *Crime and Punishment*, "Raskolnikoff's behavior . . . is a *moral* suicide, a true expiation, an exchange of a sense of Hell for a sense of Purgatory, and therefore not self-extinction."[13]

12. Andrew Sinclair, *Prohibition: The Era of Excess* (Boston: Little, Brown, 1962), p. 320.

13. Tyler, *The Hollywood Hallucination*, pp. 107–108.

But Rico Bandello reaches no moral understanding. Despite his murders and unmitigated brutality, he is shocked when mortally wounded and cannot fathom why he has been robbed of his life. He has no way to reach the articulation of a Robert Warshow, who noted that "every attempt to succeed is an act of aggression, leaving one alone and guilty and defenseless among enemies: one is *punished* for success. This is our intolerable dilemma: that failure is a kind of death and success is evil and dangerous, is—ultimately—impossible."[14]

While this message applies to both Al Capone and Rico Bandello, finally there is a point where the two gangsters part company. Capone, for all his complaints, had it infinitely better. Burnett himself offered this exalted view: "Capone is immune. He has a villa in Florida; he is a millionaire; his name has become a household word. The old pre-prohibition slogan 'you can't win' is shown to be pure nonsense."[15] But this slogan is the very essence of *Little Caesar*, the cinema's ultimate antisuccess story.

Little Caesar's dying question, "Is this the end of Rico?" is addressed desperately to "Mother of Mercy"—perhaps because he has no earthly mother. He receives no answer, but succumbs in cosmic silence, as cruel and potent as the indifferent world of the naturalistic novel.

The Production

Little Caesar was initially popular because audiences viewed the film with Al Capone in mind. Capone was "5 feet 8 inches, 190 pounds. His nose was flat; his brows dark and shaggy, and a bullet-shaped head was supported by a short thick neck."[16] All in all, this was a passable description of Edward G. Robinson—Rico Bandello on the screen—who had reached fame by playing a thinly disguised version of Capone in the 1927 Broadway play

14. Robert Warshow, *The Immediate Experience* (New York: Atheneum, 1970), p. 133.

15. W. R. Burnett, "The Czar of Chicago," *Saturday Review of Literature*, October 8, 1930, p. 240.

16. Lyle, *The Dry and Lawless Years*, p. 116.

The Racket. Robinson's earlier creation, Nick Scarsi, was an American success story, an Italian immigrant who had grown to control a criminal empire. Like Rico, Scarsi was a hard and mean killer who avoided entanglements with women. He even tried to sever a relationship between his brother Joe and a girlfriend, exactly what Rico would attempt with the affair of Joe and Olga.

Because Bartlett Cormack's play *The Racket* so resembled events in Chicago, the national company was kept from touring there by orders of Mayor William Hale Thompson's irate city fathers. Instead, *The Racket* went straight on to Los Angeles for a ten-week run, playing before the eyes of the movie industry. Paramount purchased *The Racket*, rushed it into production, and replaced Robinson with Louis Wolheim, the famed Hairy Ape of Eugene O'Neill's play. In 1929–30 Robinson played racketeer roles in *The Hole in the Wall, Night Ride, Outside the Law*, and *The Widow from Chicago*. Rico Bandello was actually Robinson's fifth gangster role in two years, but it was the one that made him famous.

How Robinson became Rico has become the stuff of Hollywood legend. Jack Warner said he talked to agent Frank Joyce about casting the lead and Joyce recommended Robinson, explaining, "We've got a client who not only looks like a gangster but he's been doing well in the Broadway hit, *The Racket*." Warner told Mervyn LeRoy about Robinson, but LeRoy wanted to cast as Rico "the young fellow with the big ears . . . in the road show of *The Last Mile*"—Clark Gable. Warner said no, and Gable went to Metro and made cinema history. Warner claimed no regrets: "I always liked and admired Gable but after seeing Edward G. Robinson in *Little Caesar*, I knew I had not made a mistake."[17]

LeRoy recalled the casting another way: "Somebody—I don't honestly remember if it was Warner or [Darryl] Zanuck or [Hal] Wallis or me—suggested . . . Robinson for the lead. Once the suggestion was made, however, all four of us immediately realized that Eddie was exactly right" (p. 94). LeRoy *never* in-

17. Warner, *My First Hundred Years in Hollywood*, p. 200.

tended Clark Gable for Rico. He wanted Gable for Joe Massara instead of Douglas Fairbanks, Jr., who did play the role. On Fairbanks: "I felt he had too much polish and urbanity. I wanted a real tough guy, not somebody who looked as though he had just stepped out of some elegant drawing room" (p. 95). LeRoy had Gable screen test by reading some of Massara's lines. Yet Zanuck led a chorus of vetoes, saying, "What the hell have you done, Mervyn? . . . You've just thrown away five hundred bucks on a test. Didn't you see the size of that guy's ears?" (p. 96).

Both the Warner and LeRoy versions of the "discovery" of Edward G. Robinson conveniently neglect the actor's blossoming film career. By late 1930, he was famous for playing gangsters in Hollywood pictures and even had grown tired of being so stereotyped. Moreover, he had already portrayed a gang leader at Warners, in the May 1930 release of *The Widow from Chicago*. Isn't it possible that Warner and LeRoy found their Rico Bandello simply by looking about the Warners lot?

In *Mervyn LeRoy: Take One*, the director of *Little Caesar* also takes credit for the screenplay, denigrating the script contributions of Lee and Faragoh; he doesn't even mention them by name: "Once the cast was set, I had to oversee the writing of the script. Hal Wallis and I did it, and it was hard. There had been nothing like it before. There were several rewrites, by several writers. They didn't seem able to grasp what we had in mind" (p. 97).

Whatever LeRoy's claim, the fact is that he kept to Faragoh's script while making *Little Caesar*. He dropped only one sequence, which Faragoh had retained from Lee's temporary script: Rico tries to turn himself in at a police station, but the cops refuse to believe the tramp before them is the infamous Little Caesar. It is interesting to see, however, how much of the *tone* of the film emanates from the final script. Faragoh's screenplay is much more sentimental than either Burnett's or Lee's *Little Caesar*, and LeRoy followed Faragoh's lead in major sections of the movie. There is much agonizing in Faragoh between Tony and his mother, as she lulls her son with memories of his childhood church (see figure 12). Also, Joe becomes hysterical each time Rico demands that he continue with the gang. "Raising his voice to a tragic pitch" (Faragoh), Joe laments the death of Tony.

Apparently Edward G. Robinson was allowed to examine Lee's first script, and he was dissatisfied, regarding it as just another gangster story. He was more pleased with a subsequent version, however, that made him think of it as a Greek tragedy in which a man defies society and is struck down by the gods and society without knowing what happened. Robinson recalled thinking of his part in the same way as if he were playing Macbeth or Richard III, trying to endow Rico with tragic stature. And Robinson's enthusiasm for his role seemed to carry over to the *Little Caesar* ensemble. "I threw myself into the shooting, and so did everybody else," LeRoy remembered. "there was a feeling that infused the whole company, a knowledge that we were creating something special. Even the extras seemed to sense it, although there were some extras who looked like they came right from the Chicago mobs. I have always thought that they probably did" (p. 97).

In *Little Caesar*, LeRoy did populate his gangs with an array of odd and interesting faces (Otero, Scabby, Vettori, Arnie Lorch, Pete Montana), worthy of the underworld creations of W. R. Burnett. He was proved correct in thinking that Douglas Fairbanks would be too epicene for the role of Joe Massara, and Olga is surely among the stiffest characterizations of Glenda Farrell's long film career. *Little Caesar* suffered the fate of numerous pictures made in the beginning years of sound: actors from the stage, unaccustomed to the demands of the film medium, went through the motions of a kind of slowed-down melodrama, making sure that the immobilized microphones picked up their awkwardly delivered lines. Furthermore, LeRoy grouped his actors as if *Little Caesar* were community theater; thus the picture suffered from an old-fashioned staginess that escaped its more smoothly cinematic contemporaries, William Wellman's *The Public Enemy* and Howard Hawks's *Scarface*.

In *Little Caesar* LeRoy did innovate in one way, often copied since: he showed violence indirectly, without actual bloodshed. "I have always been proud of one scene," LeRoy recalls. "Eddie

Robinson is talking to another hood who is wearing a distinctive diamond stickpin in his tie. 'That's a nice pin,' Eddie says. 'I'm going to have one like that someday.' I dissolved from a close-up of the pin in the hood's tie to the pin in Eddie's tie. The implication was clear—Rico knocked the guy off for his diamond stickpin—but I didn't show any killing" (p. 98). LeRoy also thought of the cigar, the prop that would be associated forever after with Edward G. Robinson. "Rico doesn't smoke cigars, until the top man in the mob offers him one. He tries to smoke it, very amateurishly, but from then on he uses them in his pathetic effort to copy the style of that top man" (p. 98).

LeRoy managed also to orchestrate at least one stirring visual sequence in *Little Caesar*, the Bronze Peacock robbery, a dynamic montage of dissolves, in the German expressionist style of Fritz Lang. Here, LeRoy learned his lesson well for his 1932 classic, *I Am a Fugitive from a Chain Gang*, which had many prolonged scenes, such as convicts breaking rocks, being chained to their beds, and escaping from the penitentiary, that depended on camera movement instead of the confinements of synchronized sound.

"The film . . . established me as a topflight director," LeRoy has boasted of *Little Caesar*. "From then on, I was noticed. Where I had been classified as a good, dependable, workmanlike director, now I was known as an innovator. . . . *Little Caesar* raised my salary by a thousand dollars a week, and now I was hot in town. Everybody wanted me" (p. 100). In truth, *Little Caesar* was an immediate smash hit, surpassing all box office records of Warners' two earlier gangster hits, *Lights of New York* (1928) and *The Doorway to Hell*. As the *New York Daily Mirror* reported on the second day of the January 1931 run: "Police reserves were summoned last night when a crowd of 3,000 persons stormed the doors of the Warner Brothers Strand Theatre at Broadway and 47th Street, soon after 3 o'clock to witness a performance . . . of *Little Caesar*. . . . The crowds stormed the two box offices and the glass in two of the doors was shattered."

Audiences were taken with the rise and fall of Rico Bandello. The 1933 sociological survey *Our Movie-Made Children* reported that many boys from the slums had identified with Rico, especially those small in stature. And critic Creighton Peet offered this first-hand account of *Little Caesar* on opening night: "This film seemed to bring out the sturdier and more aggressive members of the community who have come to see a story about how the Boy Made Good. And let me tell you that when Sergeant Flaherty's machine gun cuts him down at the end, the audience goes home mighty quiet and depressed."

Interestingly, most contemporary writers on *Little Caesar* were aware of the film's aesthetic shortcomings while praising its power as a contemporary story and Robinson's quite extraordinary performance. Typical was Mordaunt Hall's review in the *New York Times* (January 10, 1931): "The production is ordinary and would rank as just one more gangster film but for two things. One is the excellence of Mr. Burnett's credible and compact story. The other is Edward G. Robinson's wonderfully effective performance. Little Caesar becomes at Mr. Robinson's hands a figure out of Greek epic tragedy, a cold, ignorant, merciless killer, driven on and on by an insatiable lust for power, the plaything of a force that is greater than himself."

According to Mervyn LeRoy, Warners received only a few letters of complaint expressing concern over the glorification of criminality in *Little Caesar*. "Most people loved it," he says. As more and more gangster films were produced in 1931 and 1932, however, LeRoy's picture became grouped with others that angered the public. As in 1928, a wave of censorship occurred in 1932, bringing a respite from gangster films and ending in the Production Code of 1935.

Little Caesar, of course, lived on. It came back gradually on a Warners double feature with James Cagney in *The Public Enemy*, a re-release heralded in Warners' publicity as "The Two Most Ruthless Mob Monarchs Who Ever Terror-Reigned across the Screen." It has been revived countless times on television and in movie houses. And it has been written about endlessly by film historians and theorists, many of whom view the form of *Little Caesar* as the archetypal gangster genre story.

For movie fans, "Is this the end of Rico?" stands among the most famous lines in the history of the cinema. Above all, everyone admires Edward G. Robinson's larger-than-life creation of Rico Bandello. For the rest of his years, Robinson was associated with the role. Even Mervyn LeRoy gives him his due for *Little Caesar*: "The film typed Eddie, a gentle man, as a gangster for years afterward. . . . Eddie lived that part of Rico. He put in all those grunts himself—they weren't in the script and I didn't suggest them to him. He said the lines with so much authenticity that they became real; lines like 'You can dish it out but you can't take it,' 'Take him for a ride,' and 'big shot,' which all became a part of our vernacular" (p. 99).

SELECTED BIBLIOGRAPHY

Allsop, Kenneth. *The Bootleggers*. Rev. ed. New Rochelle, N.Y.: Avon, 1968.

Asbury, Herbert. *The Great Illusion: An Informal History of Prohibition*. Garden City, N.Y.: Doubleday, 1950.

Bige. "'Little Caesar.'" *Variety*, January 14, 1931, p. 30.

Burnett, W. R. "The Czar of Chicago." *Saturday Review of Literature*, October 18, 1930, p. 240.

Burnett, W. R. *Little Caesar*. New York: Dial, 1929; 2d ed., New York: Dial, 1958.

"Chicago Police Lay M'Swiggin Killing to New York Gunmen." *New York Times*, April 29, 1926.

Clarens, Carlos. *Crime Movies*. New York: Norton, 1980.

Everson, William K. *The Bad Guys*. New York: Citadel, 1964.

Faragoh, Francis Edwards. *Pinwheel*. New York: John Day, 1927.

"The Flowery End of Chicago Gangster." *Literary Digest*, December 6, 1924, pp. 34–48.

Galbraith, John Kenneth. *The Great Crash 1929*. 2d ed. Boston: Houghton Mifflin, 1961.

Kaminsky, Stuart. *American Film Genres*. Dayton, Ohio: Pflaum, 1974.

Kauffman, Stanley, with Bruce Henstell, eds. *American Film Criticism*. New York: Liveright, 1972.

Kobler, John. *Capone: The Life and World of Al Capone*. New York: Putnam, 1971.

LeRoy, Mervyn, as told to Dick Kleiner. *Mervyn LeRoy: Take One*. New York: Hawthorn, 1974.

Leuchtenburg, William E. *The Perils of Prosperity: 1914–32*. 10th ed. Chicago: University of Chicago Press, 1965.

Lyle, John H. *The Dry and Lawless Years*. Englewood Cliffs, N.J.: Prentice-Hall, 1960.

Lynn, Kenneth S. *The Dream of Success: A Study of the Modern American Imagination*. Boston: Little, Brown, 1955.

McArthur, Colin. *Underworld USA*. London: Secker and Warbur, 1971.

Merz, Charles. *The Dry Decade*. Garden City, N.Y.: Doubleday, 1931.

Nye, Russel. *The Unembarrassed Muse: The Popular Arts in America*. New York: Dial, 1970.

Peary, Gerald. "The Rise of the American Gangster Film, 1913–1930." Ph.D. dissertation. University of Wisconsin, 1977.

Peary, Gerald. "Vers une definition du 'film de gangster.'" Translated by Olivier Eyquem. *Positif*, Juillet–Aout, 1975, pp. 3–6.

Peet, Creighton. "'Little Caesar.'" *Outlook and Independent*, January 21, 1931, p. 113.

Robinson, Edward G., with Leonard Spigelgass. *All My Yesterdays*. New York: Hawthorn, 1973.

Rosow, Eugene. *Born to Lose*. New York: Oxford University Press, 1978.

Sinclair, Andrew. *Prohibition: The Era of Excess*. Boston: Little, Brown, 1962.

Skolsky, Sidney. "Putting Little Caesar on the Spot." *New Movie Magazine*, December 1930, p. 37.

Tyler, Parker. *The Hollywood Hallucination*. New York: Simon & Schuster, 1944.

Warner, Jack L., with Dean Jennings. *My First Hundred Years in Hollywood*. New York: Random House, 1964.

Warren, Harris Gaylord. *Herbert Hoover and the Great Depression*. New York: Oxford University Press, 1959.

Warshow, Robert. *The Immediate Experience*. New York: Atheneum, 1970.

Watson, Frederick. *A Century of Gunmen*. London: Nicholson & Watson, 1931.

Wecter, Dixon. *The Age of the Great Depression, 1929–1941*. 14th ed. New York: Macmillan, 1967.

1. *Rico and Joe stop for a midnight snack—and an alibi—after robbing a filling station. They are new to the big city.*

2. *The first close shot of Rico. He is envying the big-time gangsters: "Diamond Pete Montana! He don't have to waste his time on cheap gas stations."*

3. *Sam Vettori, who has just introduced Rico to the gang, endows his new thug with a nickname: "Oh, Little Caesar, huh?"*

4. *Olga is exultant when DeVoss, boss of the Bronze Peacock, decides to hire Joe as her dancing partner.*

5. *Arnie Lorch tells Rico to "Screw, mug!" when Pete Montana offers confidentialities from the Big Boy.*

6. *Rico is beginning to take over by undermining Sam's authority. Here he is reading plans he has masterminded for a robbery: "It's this layout I been figurin' out with Scabby."*

7. *Rico tells Joe, who doesn't want to take part in a robbery:* "This *is the joint where you work! Don't be forgettin' it either."*

8. *This superimposition of Rico committing the Bronze Peacock robbery ends with his disappearance from the frame, and a long shot of the gangsters, holding guns on their victims, claims the screen.*

9. *A few seconds later the camera focuses on a beastly and contorted Rico shouting, "Stand where you are, all of you."*

10. *Crime Commissioner McClure is gunned down by Rico, while onlookers react in shock.*

11. *Rico, gun drawn, hides out in the back of Vettori's with the money from the Bronze Peacock robbery.*

12. *A melodramatic moment: Tony's mama reminisces about the church that Tony attended as a boy.*

13. *Tony is shot down on the church steps by Rico, the fate of Al Capone's enemy Hymie Weiss.*

14. *Tony's funeral—probably a stock shot—is analogous to the processional through Chicago streets in 1924 after the murder of Dion O'Banion.*

15. *Rico is given a gold watch at his testimonial banquet. Symbolically, time is beginning to count for Rico.*

16. *Rico and Sam preen for a photographer at the banquet. When the camera goes off, both jump a bit, afraid of gunshots and their own perishability.*

17. *A moment before the assassination attempt, Rico buys newspapers that report on the banquet and looks at his new watch.*

18. *Otero admires Rico, dressed in formal garb for his meeting with the Big Boy.*

19. *Rico smokes and the Big Boy drinks to him, "the new boss of the North Side."*

20. *Rico threatens to murder Joe for squealing to the police, while Olga holds on desperately to her lover.*

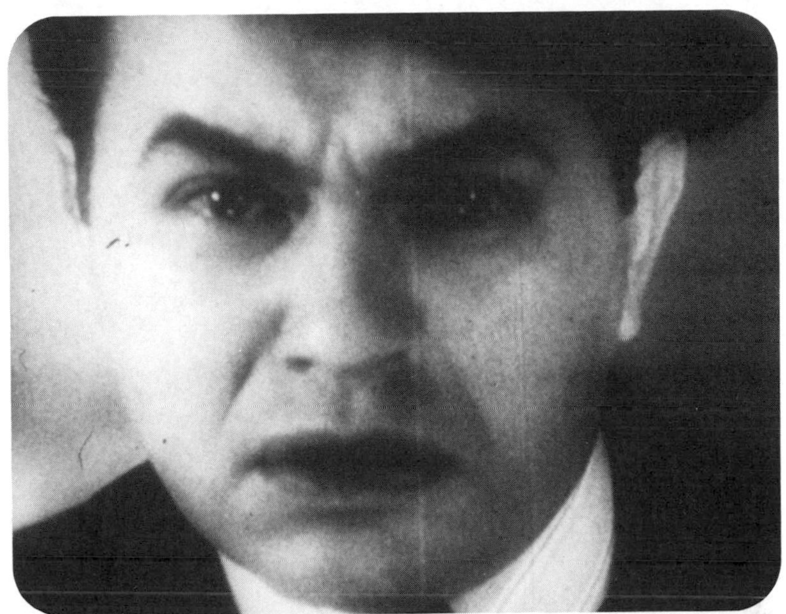

21. *Realizing he can't shoot his pal Joe, Rico loses his nerve for the first time in* Little Caesar.

22. *Ma Magdalena has hidden Rico in back of her fruit store. She will give him money, but only if "you be a good boy."*

23. *Rico guzzles alcohol in the flophouse. He is at the end of the trail.*

24. *Rico puts on his shoes before going to the telephone to threaten Sergeant Flaherty.*

25. *The decrepit figure of Rico passes a billboard announcing Joe and Olga's success. A moment later he will be shot down behind the sign.*

26. *A dying Rico mutters the immortal line: "Mother of Mercy, is this the end of Rico?"*

Little Caesar

Screenplay

by

FRANCIS EDWARDS FARAGOH

From the novel

by

W. R. BURNETT

Little Caesar

Foreword

> The first law of every being is to preserve itself and live. You sow hemlock, and expect to see ears of corn ripen.[1]
>
> —Machiavelli

FIRST SEQUENCE

1. FADE IN

EXT. FILLING STATION NIGHT MED. LONG SHOT

A closed car drives up to a filling station, the proprietor of which can be seen inside. A slight figure gets out of the car; the driver stays at the wheel with motor running. The light in the station goes out;[2] there are two or three shots in the darkness. The slight figure unhurriedly emerges from the station and steps into the front seat of the car. The door slams, the motor roars, and the car careens out of the service yard into the street on two wheels.

DISSOLVE INTO:

2. INT. LUNCH WAGON NIGHT CLOSE-UP

of a clockface with a hand turning back the clock hands from 12:05 to 11:45.

3. MED. SHOT

The clock is at the end of the lunch wagon counter. Caesar Bandello, alias Rico, drops silently from the counter on which he had been kneeling to tamper with the clock. To Joe Massara, his friend, who is seated in foreground at the counter:

RICO (with a nod of his head toward clock):
How's 'at?

JOE (grinning his appreciation):
Got to hand it to you, Rico. The old bean's working all the time.

Now a sleepy cook appears from a compartment behind the range, yawns widely, and asks:

COOK:
What'll it be, gents?

JOE (amiably):
Spaghetti and coffee for two.[3]

RICO (without directly looking at the cook):
Forget my coffee. (Silently, drawling, addressing Joe pointedly.) I don' wan' it to keep me awake. It's pretty late.

Joe nods his head significantly, indicating that he has understood Rico's purpose.

JOE (carelessly):
Oh, can't be so terrible late. (To cook.) Got a watch on you, bo?

COOK (indicates the clock):
Eleven forty-five.

JOE (also looking there):
That means quarter to twelve in any language. (Playfully poking Rico in ribs.) Well, how 'bout that java?

RICO (shrugging):
All right. Seein' as how it ain't midnight yet.

Cook nods, then goes out of picture.

4. CLOSE-UP
Rico picks up a discarded Chicago newspaper and be-

comes interested in a story. He looks with disgust at a cheap ring which he twists on the little finger of his left hand, then turns to Joe.

5. CLOSE SHOT

Rico shows the newspaper story to Joe:

INSERT HEADLINES OF STORY

Underworld Pays Respects
to Diamond Pete Montana

Joe glances swiftly at the story, looks his question at Rico:

JOE:

Well, what's that gotta do with the price of eggs?

RICO (snatching away paper):

A lot. Bit time stuff! (Musing.) "Diamond Pete Montana." He don't have to waste his time on cheap gas stations . . . *He* don't have to waste his time on hick cops . . . He's in the Big Town, doin' things in a big way.

JOE (jerking his thumb at the newspaper):

Is that what you want? A party like that for you, Rico? "Caesar Enrico Bandello Honored by His Friends"?

Rico straightens up and draws a deep breath. His jaw sets grimly as he stares into vacancy. He mutters as though talking to himself:

RICO:

I could do all the things *that* fellow does. More! When I get in a tight spot, I shoot my way out of it. Like tonight . . . sure, shoot first—argue afterwards. If you don't the other feller gets you . . . *This* game ain't for guys that's soft!

The clatter of dishes placed on the counter by the cook arouses him from his reverie. Joe attacks his food with enjoyment. Rico disregards his for the time being, studying the paper.

6. FULL SHOT

The cook comes into foreground, sits down in a chair, and leans back; he is asleep almost at once.

Rico looks up from the paper at the cook. Sure that the man is asleep, Rico slips off the stool and, with lithe swiftness, glides to the end of the counter and resets the clock.

INSERT CLOCKFACE WITH HANDS PUT FORWARD 12:15

Rico goes back to his place.[4]

7. CLOSE SHOT

Rico's face is stony as he rejoins Joe, but the latter grins at him with huge appreciation of his cleverness.

JOE (whispering):

Great!

They eat in silence for a while. Then Joe picks up his head.

JOE (wistfully):

Yeah, there's money in the Big Town, all right. And the women! Good times . . . somethin' doin' all the time . . . excitin' things. Gee, the clothes I could wear.[5] (Grasping Rico's arm with sudden seriousness; his voice becomes colored by an almost pathetic yearning.) I ain't made for this thing. Dancin' . . . that's what I wanna do.

Rico frowns. In a voice full of contempt:

RICO:

Women . . . Dancin' . . . Where do they get you? (Shakes his head violently.) I don't want no dancin'—I figure on makin' other people dance.[6]

Joe looks at him admiringly, claps him on the shoulder. There is evidently a strong feeling of friendship between them.

JOE:

You'll get there, Rico. You'll show 'em.

RICO:

Maybe. (Suddenly sits up straight. With newfound determination.) Yes, I'll show 'em! This was our last stand in this burg, Joe. We're pullin' out!

JOE (with a certain timidity):

Where we goin'?

RICO (with a vague wave of his hand):

Oh . . . east . . . That's it, east. Where things break big!

The sound of a distant police siren makes the two men prick up their ears. Sound of police siren gradually grows louder during ensuing action until the car stops outside.

Rico stands up, leaning far over the counter looking for the garbage receptacle. Spotting it, he takes the plates of spaghetti and deftly slides the remainder of the food into the pail. Sitting down, he raps loudly on the counter with his cup. Heavy-eyed with sleep, the cook stumbles to his feet and comes to them.

JOE:

More coffee, please.

The cook takes the cups and fills them at the urn. He hears the police siren and stands listening. With a shrug he turns to the counter and places the cups before the customers.

COOK:

Anything else?

JOE:

Two apple pies.

The cook shoots the pie onto the counter, then listens to the siren.

8. WIDER SHOT

The cook comes out from behind the counter and goes to the door. Rico and Joe pay no attention to him or the siren. Siren screams outside and fades away.

The cook steps aside as two cops come into the wagon. He speaks to the first. The other draws his gun and stands blocking the doorway.

COOK:

What's the matter, Charley?

The cop does not take his eyes off Rico and Joe, who swing around on their stools when he speaks.

COP:

Two cheap crooks held up a filling station on Eighth Street and shot Dinny Graham. We found their car around the corner.

COOK:

Hurt him?

COP:

Plenty!

9. CLOSE SHOT

centering on the first cop, Rico, and Joe. Joe slides off his stool, but the cop abruptly motions for him to stay where he is.

COP:

Where you guys from?

JOE:

Allendale. We didn't do nothing. Our car is out in front—the little roadster.

Joe does the talking. There is no element of fear in either his or Rico's attitude. In fact, Rico assumes a negligent pose, with one elbow on the counter, and regards the cops with subtle derision while he combs his sleek black hair of which he is inordinately proud. This is a characteristic gesture with him. He keeps the comb in his upper vest pocket; in reaching for it his hand is only an inch away from the butt of an automatic, carried in a shoulder holster.

10. WIDER SHOT (TOWARD CLOCK)

The cook, nervously afraid of the consequences of a gun battle in his place, turns to the cop. Rico and Joe look at their alibi—perhaps it will work without having to bring up the subject themselves.

COOK:

What time did it happen, Charley?

COP:

Five minutes to twelve.

The cop looks at Rico and Joe.

COP:

How long you guys been here?

COOK:

They been eating in here since 11:45.

The cop glances up at the clock in background. Pulling out his watch he compares the time. The clock is right.

COP:

Pretty lucky for them . . . If you see anybody suspicious, let me know.

The cops leave. The cook closes the door and returns to his seat behind the counter. Joe and Rico start on their pie.

11. MED. CLOSE SHOT RICO AND JOE

JOE (between mouthfuls):

Whew! That was close. You got me kinda jumpy when I seen you reachin' for the . . . (Finishes the sentence by pantomiming Rico's former action of reaching for his armpit.)

RICO (shrugs):

Maybe I should o' done it, too. (Pats his gun.) That's all I got between me and them—between me and the whole world . . . (Pushes his plate away with the half-finished pie.) Let's go.

Rico rises from his stool. The paper is still before him. Once more he looks at it. Then, with sudden decision, he quickly draws the cheap ring from his finger and throws it into a cuspidor.

INSERT FLASH OF RING DROPPING INTO CUSPIDOR

JOE:

What're you doin' that for?

RICO:

No more phonies for me . . . Big shots don't wear 'em! (On his way to door.) Ready?

Joe tosses some change on the counter as we

FADE OUT

SECOND SEQUENCE

FADE IN

CLUB PALERMO SIGN GOING ON AND OFF

DISSOLVE TO:

12. INT. SAM VETTORI'S OFFICE CLUB PALERMO CLOSE SHOT

This is a CLOSE SHOT of a game of solitaire partly laid out on a table. Two thick, heavy hands can be seen hovering over the table, placing the rest of the cards from a greasy, worn deck. Over the screen we hear (photograph Rico speaking):

RICO'S VOICE:

. . . and that's all there is to it. I beat it east, like I told you. I wanna run with your mob if you'll let me. What d'you say?

The hand goes on playing. There is silence from the owner. During this, CAMERA PANS UP to the face of Sam Vettori as he sits there still dealing the cards off the dirty deck. Sam's eyes are on the cards before him; he appears to be paying no attention to Rico, whose voice we hear again.

RICO'S VOICE (continuing; with pleading earnestness):

You won't be sorry for lettin' me in, Mr. Vettori. I'll shoot square with you . . . I'll do anything you say . . . I ain't afraid of nothin'!

Now Sam Vettori speaks. He slowly raises his eyes to the still unseen man before him as he asks:

SAM:

So you think you're a hard guy, huh?

13. INT. CLUB PALERMO SAM VETTORI'S OFFICE WIDER SHOT

Now the CAMERA includes Rico in the SHOT as he stands before Sam's table, looking at the other with a certain determination.[7]

RICO:

Gimme a chance to show you.

SAM:

What d'you know about me?

RICO:

I got told enough. How you run things this end of town. (With a wide wave of his hand which indicates the rest of the room.) 'Bout this here Club Palermo—how it's your front. I heard plenty!

SAM (placing cards):
Maybe you're good with a rod, too, huh?

RICO:
Quick with it, that's what I am. And sure.

SAM (pausing for the first time with his cards):
Well, that don't go around here. That's old stuff. This ain't the sticks.

RICO:
I get you!

Now Sam rises. Stepping closer to Rico he looks into the other's face and says in a hard, uncontradictable voice:

SAM:
All right! You stick around. But I'm the boss and I give orders. And when we split, we split my way. And no squawks. Get me?

RICO (a flash of joy lights up his face):
Sure, Mr. Vettori!

SAM (now indicating the room with his thick thumb):
Come on, meet the boys . . . They're A-1, every one of 'em . . . That's Tony Passa . . . he can drive a car better than any mug in town . . .

14. INT. SAM'S OFFICE MED. SHOT
We see Sam and Rico go toward the open door of the office. Beyond the door, not very far in the background is a gaming table with a bright droplight over it. Seated around the table are several men, some of them in shirt-sleeves, playing cards. Tony Passa, Otero, and Scabby are among them. During the walk to the door, Sam continues with a nod of his head in the direction of the table:

SAM:
. . . and that's Otero. He's the goods all right.[8] An' Scabby—what a smart guy! An' that's Killer Pepi . . .

15. CLOSE SHOT DOORWAY
into other room as Sam and Rico come in.

SAM:
Boys—I want you to meet a new guy who's gonna be with us. This is—

Boys look up from the card table, but Sam has forgotten Rico's name.

RICO:
Caesar Fredrico Bandello.

SAM (digs him playfully in ribs):
Little Caesar, eh?[9]

FADE OUT

THIRD SEQUENCE[10]

FADE IN

16. ON INSERT OF NEWSPAPER HEADLINE

New Crime Commission Head
Decrees End of Gangster Rule

Subheading:

Alvin McClure Promises Drastic
Measures against Thugs

From this,

DISSOLVE INTO:

17. INSERT IMPRESSIONISTIC SHOT OF ROULETTE WHEEL SPINNING

DISSOLVE INTO:

18. INT. ARNIE'S GAMBLING HOUSE FOYER NIGHT
We DISSOLVE in on the shadow of a hand, falling against a blank wall. The fist is closed, forefinger pointed. Hold SHOT for a second, then PAN OVER to Little Arnie, standing with Ritz Colonna. It is Arnie's hand that we see reflected in the shadow; with arm shot out, forefinger extended, he is pointing toward the gambling room, as yet unseen by the audience. Arnie, in a lowered voice, to Ritz:

ARNIE:

That's your man. I don't know who he is and I don't want to know. But he's too lucky for *my* house . . .

19. INT. LITTLE ARNIE'S GAMBLING HOUSE MAIN GAMBLING ROOM (FROM ARNIE'S ANGLE: AS HE AND RITZ SEE IT NOW)

This is the usual gambling den; card and roulette tables, etc. The whirring click of roulette wheels comes to us through the noise of a crap game in background.

20. INT. ARNIE'S GAMBLING HOUSE FOYER NIGHT

With a significant glance at Ritz, Arnie says while lowering his voice:

ARNIE:

Wait till he gets downstairs.

RITZ:

Okay, Boss! (Bending closer; in a confidential whisper.) Sam Vettori is still waiting for you in your office.

Arnie frowns, clicks his tongue with a measure of irritation.

ARNIE:

All right. I guess I'll *have* to see him. Wonder what he wants here.

With that, he turns on his heels and walks to door of his office, which is at the other end of the foyer opposite door through which we had seen the gambling room.

21. INT. ARNIE'S GAMBLING HOUSE FOYER NIGHT
CLOSE SHOT ARNIE AT DOOR

Just about to open the door, Arnie turns once more toward Ritz Colonna, who is now out of the picture, and says to him in a low voice:

ARNIE:

Say, Ritz, better stick with me! Let that other guy go—I'll need you in here. That Sam Vettori is a no good guy.

RITZ (with an understanding glance):

You said it, Boss! (Gently pushing Arnie aside.) Better let *me* go first . . . (Opens door. They enter.)

22. INT. ARNIE'S OFFICE MEDIUM SHOT

We see Sam Vettori's heavy bulk in an easy chair as Ritz enters, followed by Arnie. Rico (somewhat better dressed than in the First Sequence) is standing in a strategic position between the door and Sam. Now his hand instinctively goes toward his armpit—he is ready! But Sam waves to him as though saying, "Cut that!" Rico lowers his hand.

SAM (without rising; with a measure of amiability):

Lo, Arnie! Surprised to see me in your joint?

ARNIE:

Maybe I won't be, after you tell me what you want here.

Arnie sits down at his desk. Ritz plants himself near him, without sitting down; he is studying Rico from under drawn eyebrows. Rico stares back. Throughout this scene the two men continue to glare at each other sullenly.

SAM (bending forward in his chair):

I'll tell you all right, Arnie. Diamond Pete asked me to come up. He's coming up too.

ARNIE (surprised, but agreeably so):

Pete Montana?

SAM (nods):

That's who!

ARNIE:

Well, if Pete wants you here, it's gotta be all right with me.

Through the same door where Arnie and Ritz had come in, Diamond Pete Montana now enters with a bodyguard of his own, Kid Bean, and another mug. Montana is well dressed in a rather loud fashion and sports plenty of jewelry to live up to his sobriquet, Diamond.

Little Arnie Lorch rises from his seat behind the huge desk, and Sam Vettori also heaves his bulk out of his easy chair as Pete enters. Their manner is distinctly deferential.

Pete greets them with limp handshakes.

MONTANA:

Hello, Arnie! Hello, Vettori!

ARNIE:

How are you, Pete—how are you?

SAM:

Hello, Boss!

Montana opens his coat, loosens his muffler (it is winter and all the characters involved in this scene are wearing heavy overcoats where necessary). Arnie reaches for a box of cigars and offers it to Pete Montana, who accepts one silently. Arnie signally omits offering the box to Sam—but Sam reaches over nevertheless and takes one of the cigars.

SAM (with a touch of sarcasm):

Thanks, Arnie.

Arnie looks at him noncommittally, remains silent.

MONTANA (with an indulgent gesture, indicating the chairs to Arnie and Sam, who are still standing):

Sit down, boys. I got somethin' to tell you—a message from the Big Boy . . .

The lifted eyebrows of Sam and Arnie indicate that this is unusual and important. A certain awe is on their faces as they sit down, waiting for Montana's words. Montana perches himself on a corner of the desk.

MONTANA (warming to his speech):
Now listen, here's the lowdown . . . (He pauses dramatically, while Ernie and Sam draw their chairs nearer in listening attitudes.) The Big Boy says . . .

Rico leaves the other bodyguards standing in a group away from the desk and draws closer to the big shots. Arnie's glance falls on him. Arnie stops Montana with a wave of his hand:

ARNIE:
Just a minute, Boss! (Turning sharply to Rico.) Say, you! Nobody asked you to be buttin' into this, did they? Screw, mug!

Rico looks at him, flashing back:

RICO:
You ain't givin' me orders!

ARNIE (jumping up):
Oh! You're a fresh guy!

He starts to take a punch at Rico. Instinctively Rico's hand shoots to his armpit, but Sam quickly intervenes:

SAM (scared):
Take it easy, Rico. You wait out there for me!

RICO (shooting Arnie a glance full of hatred):
That's jake with me, Boss! (Exits.)

Arnie gives Ritz a sign. Ritz follows Rico out. Only Pete Montana's bodyguard remains on the scene near the three principals.

23. INT. ARNIE'S OFFICE CLOSE-UP MONTANA
Montana is speaking with a certain pompousness and a sense of superiority.

MONTANA:
Now listen, boys. (Bends forward, extending his forefinger as he speaks.) Watch this guy McClure—what's head of the new crime commission. He's puttin' on the screws and no mistake about it . . .

24. INT. ARNIE'S OFFICE CLOSE SHOT
Arnie and Sam listen with due solemnity, nodding their heads at each point that Montana emphasizes with his heavy fist on the desk.

MONTANA:
The Big Boy wants me to tell you to put chains on your gorillas for the next few months, 'cause if any of 'em go too far, it'll be just too bad.

ARNIE (laughs, somewhat incredulous):
He can fix anythin'. That's why he's the Big Boy.[11]

MONTANA (shaking his head):
Stop kidding yourself. Nobody can square nothin' with McClure, not even the Big Boy. Li'l jobs—that's different. We can spring guys for them. But shootin's . . .? *No sir!* (Stands up and starts to button his coat; to Sam.) It's guys like that torpedo of yours that cause all the trouble . . . (Jerks his thumb toward door where Rico had exited. Arnie grins, nods appreciatively.)

SAM:
Who, Rico? He's all right. A li'l too quick on the trigger but that's 'cause he's new.

MONTANA:
Well, it's us that'll swing with him if he shoots at the wrong time. (Pulls his derby hat down over his

eyes, starts for door. Arnie solicitously opens it for him.)

25. INT. LITTLE ARNIE'S GAMBLING HOUSE FOYER MED. CLOSE SHOT

The CAMERA is facing the door of Arnie's office. Ritz Colonna and Rico are standing there, both of their hands in their pockets, cigarettes hanging limp from the corners of their mouths. From under lowered eyelids they are watching each other in silence. Just now the door opens and Montana exits, followed by Arnie, Sam, and Montana's bodyguard.

MONTANA:

Now remember what I told you. (He struts to door, stops in front of Rico. Surveys him with a hard glance.) And you—you take it easy with that cannon.

26. INT. LITTLE ARNIE'S GAMBLING HOUSE FOYER CLOSE-UP

Rico looks at the great Pete Montana with adulation, then his expression changes to harshness. His eyes drop from Montana's face. Through the shot we hear:

MONTANA:

You hear me?

27. INT. LITTLE ARNIE'S GAMBLING HOUSE FOYER CLOSE-UP PETE MONTANA (FROM RICO'S ANGLE)

His glance stops at a large horseshoe pin in Montana's cravat, then drops to a large flashy ring (we use this ring later).

RICO (meekly):

Yes, Mr. Montana!

28. INT. LITTLE ARNIE'S GAMBLING HOUSE FOYER MED. CLOSE SHOT

With a lordly gesture, Montana takes his leave, his bodyguard following him.

MONTANA:

S'long, boys.

OTHERS (ad lib):

Good night.

Montana and his bodyguard walk out of the picture. Little Arnie turns to Rico to say with a malicious sidelong glance at Vettori:

ARNIE:

Leave your gat home on the pianna next job you pull. Yeah, park it next to your milk bottle!

Rico hardens again. Sam swings around, growling:

SAM:

G'wan! Run your own mob, Arnie—I'll take care of mine!

There is no love lost between him and Arnie. The latter starts to make a sharp retort, but Rico steps up to him, smiling evilly:

RICO:

Yeah, I'll park it! I don't need no cannon to take care of guys like you, Mr. Lorch. (Turns, follows Sam.)

29. INT. LITTLE ARNIE'S GAMBLING HOUSE FOYER CLOSE-UP
On Little Arnie, who stares blankly after Rico muttering:

ARNIE:

He's gonna get up in this world—yes he will! A couple feet higher than he wants to—if the rope don't break . . .[12]

FADE OUT

FOURTH SEQUENCE

FADE IN

30. INT. BRONZE PEACOCK FULL SHOT NIGHT

Through a menu heading—The Bronze Peacock—we DISSOLVE INTO:

FULL SHOT of the main room in the Bronze Peacock, a smart North Side nightclub. The room is richly decorated in excellent taste; the guests are mostly in dinner clothes. A good orchestra is playing a dance number. A number of people are dancing. There is general movement of waiters, guests, etc.

31. INT. BRONZE PEACOCK MED. SHOT DANCE FLOOR TRUCK

On the dance floor. Prominent in foreground are Joe and Olga Stassoff, dancing. As they come into CAMERA we pick them up and follow them in a CLOSE-UP.

Joe is immaculately dressed in tails. Olga wears a stunning evening gown. The girl looks up at the boy with a melting expression in her eyes.

OLGA (softly):

> Gee, I thought you weren't coming at all! I kept on looking at that door and saying to myself: "He forgot all about me . . ." (But she smiles at him as though courting his reassuring denial.)

Joe smiles back at her.

JOE:

> Not a chance, Baby! Wouldn't I be a sap to miss out on such a swell break—'specially with a dame like you for a partner?

OLGA:

> We oughta make a swell team, you and me. That's what I told my agent, too, when he brought you 'round. (Pressing his arm; anxiously.) Do your best, will you, Joe? The manager is eyeing you up. I want him to like you.

JOE:

Just watch me! He's gonna get an eyeful.

32. INT. BRONZE PEACOCK CLOSE SHOT

On DeVoss standing near the dressing room entrance. DeVoss is a sleek maître d'hôtel, proud of his establishment. He is closely following the movements of the young couple. DeVoss smiles his approval.

33. INT. BRONZE PEACOCK LONG SHOT DANCE FLOOR

Toward Joe and Olga from DeVoss's angle. The music rises to a crescendo and Joe, taking advantage of a clear spot on the floor, executes a graceful movement ending in a spin.

The orchestra stops. There is desultory hand clapping for another encore, then the dancers drift toward their tables.

Joe and Olga head for DeVoss. (This shot allows the use of doubles if necessary.)

34. INT. BRONZE PEACOCK CLOSE SHOT DANCE FLOOR

On DeVoss as Joe and Olga enter to meet him. Olga is breathing quickly after her exertions. She is holding Joe's hand and pulls him to DeVoss, questioning eagerly.

OLGA:

Well, I got hold of a real hoofer for a partner, didn't I, Mr. DeVoss?

DeVoss runs an appraising eye from Joe's glossy hair to his immaculate boots. There is no question but what Joe has it. But he stalls, teasing the girl. Olga is on tenterhooks and says pleadingly:

OLGA:

He's an elegant dancer. We'd panic 'em, working together.

DeVoss smiles at her.

DEVOSS:

You're not trying to sell him now, Olga? (Laughs; to Joe.) Well, young fellow, a hundred a week ought to buy you. That's more than I usually start them with.

JOE (laughing):

Can't get no limousines with that, but it ought to buy me a bit of gas till I get paid enough to buy a car to it.

Olga looks at the two men, delighted. DeVoss laughs.

OLGA:

Gee, thanks, Mr. DeVoss! You won't be sorry for this.

DEVOSS (chucking Olga under the chin):

Olga, when are you going to give me a chance to do something I *can* be sorry for?

Olga takes Joe's arm and leads him toward the dressing room. DeVoss looks after them, then turns to a captain who enters.

35. INT. BRONZE PEACOCK DRESSING ROOM FULL SHOT

Joe and Olga come into the girl's dressing room, which they share from now on. It is a cozy place with a dressing table, day bed, a chair or two. Pictures of a few movie stars are on the wall.

Joe is smiling over his success and starts to sit down, but Olga stops him. Her manner undergoes a decided change. She holds him by the lapels of his coat and looks up.

36. INT. BRONZE PEACOCK DRESSING ROOM CLOSE SHOT OLGA

as she studies the boy narrowly.

OLGA:

So it's you and me from now on. Well, I'm glad and

I ain't ashamed to tell you. It's no use kidding . . . I guess you know by this time how I feel about you. That's all right with you, isn't it? (Her voice softens, an anxious note creeps into it.) Or have you got another girl? A steady, I mean?

37. INT. BRONZE PEACOCK DRESSING ROOM MED. CLOSE SHOT INCLUDING BOTH

Joe looks at her steadily and laughs provocatively.

JOE:

Hundreds of 'em. Sure! Only . . . (suddenly putting his arms around her) what's the difference? This is gonna be real, huh? We'll make it . . . mean something . . .

OLGA (softly):

Yeah, Joey. Let's!

JOE:

'Cause I need somebody . . . somebody like you . . . awful bad . . . Do you believe me, Olga?

OLGA:

I want to believe you . . .

38. INT. BRONZE PEACOCK DRESSING ROOM MED. CLOSE SHOT

Joe takes the girl in his arms and kisses her. Olga's arms go around him. In doing this, she touches the gat under his left arm and draws away. Pointing to the gun, she asks, frightened:

OLGA:

What's that? What you got there, Joe?

Joe casually takes the big automatic from its holster and slips it into the dressing table drawer. Olga's eyes go wide at sight of the gun. She whispers:

OLGA:

What are you doing with that?

Joe stares at her grimly, takes her by both arms, and pulls her face close to his, saying:

JOE:

Can't you forget you seen it? It won't make no difference . . . not between us, Olga. Don't you worry, Babyface. It's just a little good-luck charm I carry with me . . .

Olga wets her lips and nods. Joe releases her. The girl looks at him with a different expression now—there is a glint of frightened admiration in her eyes, but she speaks stubbornly:

OLGA:

That your racket?

JOE (uneasy, but with a smile on his face):

Maybe . . .

OLGA:

I suppose I got no right to ask you. But now that we got an understanding . . . Joe, couldn't you . . . leave it . . . ? (Shakes her head bravely as though speaking the words to herself.) No, I suppose I *haven't* got the right . . .

JOE:

What would be the good of you asking, Kiddy? Once in a gang . . . you know the rest . . .

OLGA (with all the confidence of her love):

I don't want to know. Maybe it can be different this time—if we try . . .

JOE:

I never seen the guy could get away with it . . .

She places her head against his shoulder. He puts his arm around her.

FADE OUT

FIFTH SEQUENCE

FADE IN

39. INSERT ELECTRIC SIGN

C L U B
P
A
L
E
R
M
O
DANCING

DISSOLVE THROUGH THIS SIGN TO:

FULL SHOT OF VETTORI'S OFFICE
(The Club Palermo in Little Italy belongs to Sam Vettori. An upstairs room is the headquarters of the gang. We need a corner of the cafe proper, a passageway through the kitchen to the stairs—the upstairs office with closet and concealed sliding panel leading to back stairs and alley.)

Sam Vettori, as usual, is sitting at a table playing a game of solitaire. Grouped around him are Otero, Killer Pepi, and Tony Passa. (Tony is boyish; Otero has the perfect poker face—he is a little Mexican; Killer Pepi is a huge, hairy, ferocious Sicilian.)

Leaning against another table, which is at some distance from Sam's, is Rico. It is significant that he is standing alone, keeping apart from the group that has gathered around Vettori. And during the early part of scene, while the rest of the gang are intent on Sam's words, Rico continues to study a sheet of paper, which is in his hand.

40. INT. VETTORI'S OFFICE CLOSER SHOT GROUP
Sam, placing the cards, continues a conversation apparently begun some time ago.

SAM:

But we gotta be careful. Little Arnie is interested in this here club and if it gets out who pulled the job . . .

PEPI (interrupting):

Aw, nobody will be wise to us! They're careless 'cause they never been tapped.

SAM (uneasily):

Just the same, I don't like this whole business.

TONY (very nervously):

I don't neither, Sam! Cross my heart I don't. (Looking around with instinctive fear.) I couldn't sleep last night . . . I was that worried . . . I don't wanna take chances—not now, the way they're closin' down on us . . .

41. INT. VETTORI'S OFFICE CLOSE-UP RICO

He looks up from his paper; a sneering expression comes over his face as he turns on Tony:

RICO:

What's the matter, Tony? Gettin' yellow?

42. INT. VETTORI'S OFFICE MED. SHOT INCLUDING RICO IN SHOT

Tony bristles, flashes an anxious glance at Rico—but his eyes droop under the steely scrutiny of the other.

TONY (whining):

Aw, it ain't that . . . only . . . well, gee whiz, none of us want to hang, do we?

RICO (firmly):

You'd like to quit, wouldn't you? You'd like to run out on us, wouldn't you? You're yellow, you dirty . . . (Takes a step toward Tony, who retreats, his eyes wide with fear.)

Sam who has been watching this scene from under lowered eyebrows, now barks at Rico:

SAM:

Hold on, Rico!

Rico reluctantly stops.

SAM (glowering):

Where'd you get that yellow stuff? If you're so anxious to know who's yellow, I'll tell you. It's Joe Massara, your pal. That's why he didn't show up tonight.

RICO (savagely):

Joe'll be here. Just 'cause he's late . . .

SAM (waves):

Yeah, I know all about it. Well, I'll just give him ten minutes more . . . Then we'll see . . . (Pulls out his heavy gold watch and glances at it. Rico steps up to the table, plants himself in front of Sam.)

RICO:

Listen, Sam. Joe is all right. He's the best front man in the world. He can go into a swell hotel and order a suite—a suite—and it's all right. Without Joe we can't pull this job and you know it.

During this speech, Rico has been emphasizing his remarks by fluttering the sheet of paper in his hand. Sam, who had been more concerned with his cards than with listening to Rico's speech, now looks up. Narrowing his eyes, he asks Rico:

SAM:

What's that paper?

43. INT. VETTORI'S OFFICE MED. CLOSE SHOT RICO AND SAM

RICO:

It's this layout I been figurin' out with Scabby . . .

SAM:

This here nightclub job?

RICO:

Yeah.

SAM (amiably):

Let's see it a minute!

Unsuspecting, Rico hands over the document. Sam, without looking at it, suddenly rips the paper in two and throws it on the floor. Rico's face darkens, his fists clench.

SAM:

Until I say different, nobody's goin' to plan for this mob but me. Savvy?

Rico stands for a second, glowering. It seems as though he were to spring at Sam the next moment. Then he drops his hands, turns away, and walks out of picture.

44. INT. VETTORI'S OFFICE MED. SHOT

Sam laughs, looks up at the gangsters around the table as though seeking their support, but the men seem embarrassed, ill at ease. Only Tony forces a weak smile. In background Rico is seen striding to the door, which is heavy and has a shutter in it. We see Rico going out through the door. Sam resumes his cards, saying:

SAM:

Now get on to this . . . You, Tony, will handle the bus and . . .

45. INT. CLUB PALERMO STAIRCASE (LEADING FROM MAIN FLOOR TO SAM'S OFFICE)

Rico, having come out of door, is now standing at the head of the staircase, anxiously peering down the steps. For a while he is alone, then Joe comes leaping up the stairs, skipping two at a time. Joe is dressed in a form-fitting, velvet-collared, blue overcoat, his natty derby hat at an angle.

JOE:

Hello, Rico.

With a wide grin of greeting he shoots out his hand. But Rico disregards this, as he says:

RICO:

I told you to be here at eight-thirty.

JOE (obviously not telling the truth):

Well . . . you see . . . I was busy . . . rehearsing and . . . you know how it is!

RICO (darkly):

Yeah, I know how it is! They've been sayin' it in there . . . (Jerks his thumb in direction of door.) Only I didn't believe 'em, see! They're crazy when they call you—*yellow!* (He says the last word with significance, looking hard at Joe.)

JOE (nervously; with an abrupt movement of his hand, as though waving aside the accusation):

Aw, tell 'em to . . .

He doesn't finish the sentence. With sudden anxiety in his voice, he bends closer to Rico.

JOE:

What's the big rush for, anyway?

46. INT. CLUB PALERMO STAIRCASE CLOSE SHOT RICO AND JOE

RICO (affecting a careless manner, though with a sharp, hard expression on his face):

It's a li'l job we need you for. A li'l job at the—Bronze Peacock. (Again there is sinister emphasis on the last two words; he is watching Joe's face closely.)

JOE (his mouth drops open, eyes dilated; he backs up a step):

What do you men? You kidding me or something? (Feverishly grasping Rico's arm.) But how can I take the chance? They're my friends—everybody knows me.

RICO (coldly):

That's why! Nobody will suspect *you*. Don't stall, Joe.

JOE (desperately):

I ain't stallin'! You gotta let me out of it, Rico. You gotta. I don't want to . . . I'm workin' steady . . . can't a guy ever say he's *through?*

RICO (carefully measuring his words):

You're gonna be in on it and you'll like it. The time is to be sharp midnight on New Year's Eve.

JOE (with almost a shriek):

I won't . . . I can't. (Instantly cringing as Rico pushes his face closer to him. A cunning note comes into Joe's voice.) I can't . . . don't you see . . . ? I'll . . . gee, I'll be workin' New Year's Eve . . .

RICO (straightens with a curious gleam in his eyes and says with a nod toward the door):

This is the joint where you work! Don't be forgettin' it either . . . (Turns to door, over his shoulder commands.) Come on!

Joe, pale, quaking, follows him.

47. INT. SAM VETTORI'S OFFICE CLOSE SHOT

This is the group again. Sam is still dealing the cards; now he looks up.

SAM:

Maybe it ain't so hot, though. Maybe we can't buck Little Arnie.

At this point Rico walks into the picture, with Joe a step behind him.

RICO:

I can.

SAM (shrugs):

You're too good, that's what. (Now he notices Joe.) You were in a hurry to get here all right. Maybe this kinda work ain't to your liking, huh?

Joe lowers his eyes, bites his lips. Rico hastily answers for him.

RICO:

Joe is all right, Sam. He's in with us.

Again he looks sharply at Joe. Joe feels the challenge of the eyes, looks up, then turns his eyes away once more answering in a low voice:

JOE:

Yeah, I'm in with you . . .

48. INT. VETTORI'S OFFICE CLOSE-UP SAM

With an energetic movement unusual to him, Sam suddenly shoves the cards off the table. Reaching in his pocket, he produces a rolled-up map.

SAM:

Well, let's see . . . Here's the way I doped out this thing . . . (Slides the map on the table. Lays his thick forefinger on it. Then he looks at Rico.) I—Sam Vettori! Not you, Rico . . . nor nobody else . . . that's clear, ain't it?

49. INT. VETTORI'S OFFICE MED. CLOSE SHOT GROUP

Some of them are bent over the table. Only Rico is

standing, his manner aloof as he looks down on the plan. There is the semblance of a cynical smile on his lips. Joe is also at some distance from the table, nervously lighting a cigarette.

SAM (now poking the plan with his finger):
Here's where you stand, Otero . . . This is your spot, Killer . . . Rico is over here . . . That's plain, ain't it?

RICO:
Sure! Only . . . (With a definite sneer now, he pokes a quick finger at the paper.) Who stands here? Yeah, the back door . . . ? Kinda forgot that, didn't you?

From Sam's puzzled face, we can guess that he is caught unaware. He scratches his head, then takes out his fury on Rico.

SAM:
I'm still bossin' this job, you . . . One more crack outa you . . .

50. INT. VETTORI'S OFFICE OTERO AND TONY
Otero, grinning widely, pokes Tony in the ribs. With a wink:

OTERO:
Big smart guy, Rico. Lotta brain, you betcha my life . . .

TONY (with a nervous half-smile):
Yeah, but I'm scared, Otero, honest to goodness I'm scared . . .

OTERO:
You craz'. Rico, he come with us . . .

51. INT. VETTORI'S OFFICE MED. CLOSE SHOT OF THE GROUP
Sam is continuing:

SAM:

You, Joe, will be in the lobby at five minutes after twelve . . .

52. INT. VETTORI'S OFFICE CLOSE-UP OF JOE

as he is listening to Sam, whose words come over the screen:

SAM'S VOICE:

And give us the high sign if everything's okay.[13]

Joe's face twitches. Instinctively he opens his coat and starts fingering his holster, which is significantly empty just now.

DISSOLVE INTO:

53. INT. BRONZE PEACOCK DRESSING ROOM CLOSE-UP JOE

His figure of the preceding SHOT DISSOLVES into this one—in exactly the same position. But now Joe is dressed in tails again and his hand, which had been examining the empty holster in the former SHOT, is now slipping a gun into it. The revolver in its place, he draws his coat tight over it.

54. INT. BRONZE PEACOCK DRESSING ROOM MED. SHOT

We now see that Joe is alone—Olga is not in the room. With a last glance in the mirror, and a final adjustment of his tie, Joe crosses to door, opens it, and slips out.

CUT TO:

55. INT. BRONZE PEACOCK MAIN ROOM MED. CLOSE SHOT

Little Arnie is entertaining a party of friends at a prominent table near the dance floor. DeVoss is in the background. The noise has materially increased with the approach of New Year. Decorations, appropriate to the New Year. Signs and transparencies. "Happy New Year" prominently displayed. Little Arnie's friends are a vulgar, boisterous lot. They are drinking champagne. Arnie feels important and is a trifle tight.

56. INT. BRONZE PEACOCK MAIN ROOM CLOSER SHOT
Little Arnie's woman—known as Blondy Belle—wants to propose a toast but no one will listen to her. She nudges Arnie. The gambler shouts authoritatively.

ARNIE:
Ho! Let's have quiet, gang. Blondy's gonna give a toast!

ANOTHER VOICE:
Sssh! Blondy's gonna turn a new leaf . . .

A DRUNKEN VOICE:
Yeah, a loose leaf.

The bunch at the table stop their gabble and turn bleary eyes on the blonde who tries to stand up, thinks better of it, and speaks her piece from her chair.

BLONDY:
Here's to the guy what invented New Year's! And here's to Little Arnie—may he never be left in the Lorch!

This bon mot is greeted with a shout of laughter. Blondy grins with pride at the reception accorded her wit. Arnie slaps her on the back as he would a man, then pulls out a huge role of bills and gives her fifty.

ARNIE:
Here—catch!

BLONDY:
Dollink! May you never die—much!

After this magnanimous gesture he looks around the club. The entrance of a party on the other side of the dance floor catches his eye, and he turns squarely around in his chair to see better.

57. INT. BRONZE PEACOCK MAIN ROOM MED. LONG SHOT
from Arnie's angle on a party of three men and two la-

dies who are sitting down at the table across the dance floor.

58. INT. BRONZE PEACOCK MAIN ROOM CLOSER SHOT
on same group. They are middle-aged, quietly dressed with an air of authority and culture. The host is a big, distinguished-looking man with iron gray hair and firm, clean cut jaw. His name is Alvin McClure and he is head of the crime commission. One of the ladies is his wife.

59. INT. BRONZE PEACOCK MAIN ROOM CLOSE SHOT
on Little Arnie who is talking to DeVoss. Blondy is in scene, listening.

ARNIE (pointing):

Holy Moses, lamp McClure . . . the crime commission buzzard. Bring 'im over and I'll buy 'im a lemonade!

DeVoss doesn't like the idea at all and tries politely to dissuade Arnie.

DeVOSS:

Some other time, Arnie.

BLONDY (nastily butting in):

Go on, DeVoss, do as you're told or we'll wreck your gilded joint. Maybe we ain't good enough to associate with those high-hat mugs . . . ?

60. INT. BRONZE PEACOCK MAIN ROOM CLOSE SHOT
centering on DeVoss and McClure. McClure greets the nightclub proprietor as a friend—DeVoss tries to be ingratiating.

McCLURE:

Good evening, DeVoss. Quite a party.

DeVOSS:

Thank you, Mr. McClure. Er—er—Mr. Lorch, one

of my financial backers, would like very much to meet you. May I bring him over?

McClure frowns thoughtfully—the name is vaguely familiar.

McCLURE:

Lorch? Lorch? (He straightens with a jerk, demanding coldly.) I didn't understand that persons of his type were connected with this place. (Rising.) I'm sorry, Mr. DeVoss, but you might inform "Mister" Lorch that we're—leaving! I came to this place under a misapprehension, obviously.

The ladies start to gather their wraps, McClure impatiently helping them.

FIRST LADY (obviously his wife):

Alvin, dear, isn't it a bit extreme to get into such a huff . . . ? We're being rather conspicuous . . .

McCLURE (irritably):

Do you expect me to fraternize with crooks?[14]

61. INT. BRONZE PEACOCK MAIN ROOM CLOSE SHOT
on DeVoss, Little Arnie, and Blondy.

BLONDY (a glass poised in her hand, ready to throw it at DeVoss):

Well, where is the guardian angel?

DeVOSS (agitated):

Say, Arnie, I certainly put my foot in it. McClure is leaving!

ARNIE:

Yeah? Well, let 'im go and take a flying jump at the moon!

INSERT COMPOSITE SHOT OF WHISTLE BLOWING. THEN ANOTHER AND ANOTHER UNTIL THE SCREEN IS FULL OF THEM. A NEW YEAR IS BORN.

The sound of the whistles makes Blondy forget the quarrel. She lets out a yell and grabs Arnie around the neck, giving him a sloppy kiss.

BLONDY:

Happy New Year and see how you like it!

DeVoss ducks in the excitement.

62. INT. BRONZE PEACOCK MAIN ROOM FULL SHOT

of the room. The air is filled with confetti and serpentine. The noise is terrific, practically drowning out the whistles from outside.

INSERT CLOCK, HANDS POINTING TO 11:55

63. INT. BRONZE PEACOCK FOYER FULL SHOT

Joe is standing at the top of the steps leading to the main room. He draws the heavy curtains, partially shutting out the racket from inside. Turning, he glances coolly around. The only people here are employees—two check girls, a waiter, a cashier, and a cigar clerk. Joe starts for the cigar counter.

64. INT. BRONZE PEACOCK FOYER CLOSE SHOT ON CHECK GIRLS

One of the check girls watches Joe with longing eyes and remarks to her coworker:

CHECK GIRL:

Gosh! That Joe Massara is a hot-looking guy.

The other nods her agreement.

SECOND CHECK GIRL (with eyes rolled skyward):

Mmm! Yum—yum!

65. INT. BRONZE PEACOCK FOYER MED. CLOSE SHOT CIGAR COUNTER

Joe stands beside the waiter, who is getting cigars for a

party inside. The clerk looks at Joe while the waiter picks up the cigars.

JOE:

A package of Egyptian Ovals. Make 'em tobacco!

He flips a dollar bill on the counter. The waiter looks up at the spendthrift—these cigarettes are expensive. The clerk sticks his head in the case, fishing for the cigarettes. Joe and the waiter have their backs to the door.

66. INT. BRONZE PEACOCK FOYER TRUCK SHOT ON MAIN DOOR

With Rico slightly in the lead, the three gunmen come through the front door. Their overcoat collars are turned up, their mufflers shroud the lower halves of their faces, and hats are pulled down so only the eyes show. Rico has his automatic in his hand. Otero prominently displays the evil-looking shotgun. Tony carries a gun and some canvas sacks. We TRUCK BACK as they come into the room and separate fanwise. Rico makes for the office door. Tony the cashier and Otero stay near the entrance.

67. INT. BRONZE PEACOCK FOYER CLOSE SHOT

Joe wheels around, throws his hands into the air as if on a signal, and yells:

JOE:

It's a holdup!

The waiter turns and nearly collapses, his tray falling with a clatter. The clerk staggers back against the wall. In background we see the hands of the check girls pop into the air.

RICO (out of scene):

A mind reader, ain't you? Well, keep 'em steady!

NOTE: We see nothing of the gunmen with the victims. They are always just out of scene except perhaps for the muzzle of a gun, a hand, or their shadows. We must handle this very carefully to avoid censorship.

68. INT. BRONZE PEACOCK FOYER CLOSE-UP PAN SHOT
on the cashier, an elderly, frightened man. His hands are above his head; he gasps like a fish. Tony's voice, trying to be tough, is heard out of scene:

TONY:

Fork over, Pop, fork over.

The cashier lowers his hands and we PAN DOWN to see him commence dumping money into a canvas sack held by Tony. Only the latter's hands are in scene.

69. INT. BRONZE PEACOCK FOYER CLOSE SHOT
DeVoss's assistant, a Czech with a swarthy complexion, appears in the door of the office. A look of incredulous amazement sweeps over his face and his hands leap up. He slumps against the doorjamb. Rico's shadow comes into scene beside the Czech and we hear his voice:

RICO (out of scene):

Quick, you! I want a look in there.

70. INT BRONZE PEACOCK MAIN FLOOR TRUCK SHOT
A drunk comes in the door and we follow him. He evidently runs smack into Otero and his shotgun. A lugubrious expression comes into his face; he bows and takes off his silk hat. Then his hands go into the air, and he sidles along to back up against the wall, trying hard to keep his balance.

DRUNK (while putting up hands; with a beatific expression):

Very—happy—New—Year . . . !

71. INT. BRONZE PEACOCK FOYER CLOSE SHOT
on Joe and the waiter. Joe is quite brave, even to the point of kidding. He speaks loudly:

JOE:

Wow—a nice little celebration we're having! Fine little celebration . . .

He smiles at the waiter, who looks hastily away with agonized eyes as if to say to Otero: "I can't help what that bird's saying."

72. INT. BRONZE PEACOCK FOYER CLOSE SHOT
on Otero near the door as Tony backs into scene. The boy has the money sacks under one arm. The other hand swings a gun unsteadily around the arc of the room. Otero is a statue; only his quick piercing eyes move. Tony is gradually losing his nerve.

73. INT. BRONZE PEACOCK FOYER CLOSE SHOT
Rico backs out of the office door, stuffing a wad of bills in his overcoat pocket; his pockets bulge. He snaps the door shut, then whips around and runs into scene.

74. INT. BRONZE PEACOCK FOYER MED. SHOT
The McClure party come through the curtains from the main room and stops, petrified. We hear Rico's intimidating voice:

RICO (out of scene):

Stand right there! All of you!

Two of the men and both women put up their hands; McClure hesitates. Suddenly one of the ladies faints and falls, hitting her head with an audible thump, and slips down the steps. This is too much for McClure, who gives a bellow of rage and reaches for a gun.

McCLURE:

You dirty, low-down . . .

A gun roars out of scene. McClure takes a couple of steps, a dazed expression on his face, and pitches forward, arms outflung.[15]

75. INT. BRONZE PEACOCK MAIN DOOR CLOSE SHOT
Tony is gone. Otero is holding the door open for Rico, who is slowly backing to him, his gun raised, a feral expression on his face. There is no doubt as to who fired the shot. Rico whisks through the door. They vanish.

76. INT. BRONZE PEACOCK FULL SHOT REVERSE ANGLE
A woman screams. Everyone rushes for McClure. A crowd forms around him. Joe beats it for the back of the building. Confusion!

77. EXT. BRONZE PEACOCK NIGHT CLOSE SHOT
on Tony, who has already started the car. Tears are streaming down his face. He is completely unnerved. Otero is on the running board, holding the door open for Rico, who barges into scene.[16] Tony cannot get the gears meshed. Rico slaps him hard across the face.

RICO:

What's the matter, losing your nerve?

The boy shivers—a single sob escapes him—but the blow acts like a dash of cold water. He throws the gears into second and the car leaps away.

78. INT. BRONZE PEACOCK DRESSING ROOM MED. SHOT
Olga is in her dressing room when Joe staggers through the door. Joe's face is chalk-pale, his hair disarrayed.

OLGA:

What's the matter? Joe . . . what happened?

Joe supports himself with one hand on dressing table. He is scared through and through.

JOE:

It's all right . . . nothing . . . (Trying to compose himself, forcing a certain calmness which doesn't quite come off.) The joint's been held up . . . They . . . they shot McClure!

OLGA (with frantic fear in her voice):

JOE!

JOE (with a faint, painful smile):

Well . . . now you know . . . (He drops into a chair.)

Olga, drawing back, stares at him in horror.

OLGA (quaking):

It was you . . .

Joe's face distorts under the direct accusation. He jumps as if to rush at her, as if to force her to be quiet.

JOE:

NO . . . that's a lie . . . I . . .

OLGA (her voice harsher now):

You shot McClure!

JOE (his face twitching with fear):

I didn't . . . I swear I didn't. It wasn't me that shot him—it was . . .

But before he can complete the sentence, he catches himself, shuts his eyes, with lips compressed as though to choke back the truth. Then his hands drop inertly to his sides and he mutters:

JOE:

I don't know who . . . (Picking up his head with a certain bravado.) But it's our hips for this job, all right![17]

With that, he gets to the drawer, pulls it open, hastily drops revolver into it, again shutting drawer. But he hasn't the energy to leave the dressing table this time. He just stands there staring at his own image in the mirror.

79. INT. BRONZE PEACOCK DRESSING ROOM CLOSE SHOT

The CAMERA faces the mirror at such an angle that Joe's body is excluded from the SHOT—only his face is visible, as reflected by the mirror. His eyes stare ahead of him, full of hopelessness and misery. After a while Olga comes up behind him, places her arm around his neck. We now see her face also in the mirror, cheek pressed close to Joe's.

OLGA:

Maybe everything will be all right Joey . . . Maybe he wasn't hurt badly! But you're through with that bunch! You don't belong, Joe . . . you're not that kind. You'll never go near them again.

JOE (sadly shaking his head):

You can't go back on the gang!

FADE

SIXTH SEQUENCE

80. INT. PALERMO OFFICE MED. SHOT FADE IN

In foreground stands Vettori, mopping his face with his bandana and looking at Rico, who is emptying his pockets of money. It is quite a pile; he adds the contents of the canvas sacks to it.

In background Otero locks the riot gun in the closet—which holds a regular arsenal—then takes off his overcoat, unconcernedly walks to the table, and sits down.

81. INT. PALMERO OFFICE CLOSE SHOT

Vettori senses something wrong. There is nothing jubilant in the attitude of these two men. They should be gay after a successful job.

SAM (sweating with excitement):
Well? Well? Everything go off all right? Tell us, for the love of . . .

RICO (without looking up from counting the money):
Sure all right! I had to take care of a guy.

Vettori falls into a chair with a thump as though his legs had suddenly lost their strength. His eyes bulge; his face grows purple with rage.

SAM:
A guy? Who—who—was it?

RICO:
McClure!

82. INT. PALMERO OFFICE CLOSE-UP VETTORI
Sam appears to be having an apoplectic seizure. Inarticulate, he bangs on the table with both hands. Finally he manages to gasp with hoarse rage:

SAM:
What did I tell you, Rico? Didn't I say to make it clean? Didn't I say no gunwork? You . . . you . . . Amore de dio . . . (Chokes with rage.)[18]

83. INT. PALMERO OFFICE CLOSE SHOT
White with anger, Rico replies:

RICO:
You think I'm gonna let a guy pull a gat on *me?* He tried to get me! See? That's the way you gotta play this game.

Vettori makes an elaborate, tragic gesture, rocking in his chair as if in pain.

SAM (wringing his hands):
The head of the crime commission! The Big Boy can't do us no good—not this trip. They'll get us dead sure now . . . What am I gonna do?

84. INT. PALMERO OFFICE MED. SHOT
Rico continues automatically to count the money. Over his shoulder, without looking up:

RICO:

Maybe you better go and give yourself up. You're slippin', Sam.

SAM (still too frantic to react to the insult, he is suddenly reminded of something and asks, his voice trembling):

And Tony? What'd you do with Tony? Where is he?

OTERO (answering him):

Gettin' rid of the car—Tony nervous . . . bigga baby, Tony . . .[19]

CUT TO:

85. EXT. ALLEY FULL SHOT
This is a dark alley, only faintly illumined by a solitary streetlamp. Tony's car drives up and into the scene, veering dangerously. All at once something seems to go wrong with it; it swerves to the curb and comes to a dead halt as the engine dies.

86. INT. CAR CLOSE SHOT TONY AT WHEEL
His face twitching with terror, Tony is seen fumbling with the gearshift. But his hands shake so that he is unable to mesh the gears. Again and again he tries. Now he is sobbing aloud—his whole body is shaken—then abandoning his task in panic, he quickly yanks the door open and starts running down the street.

87. EXT. ALLEY TRUCK SHOT
THE CAMERA TRUCKS with Tony as he runs, flattened against the walls of the building, his knees giving way under him, his loud sobbing increasing as he staggers along.

CUT BACK TO:

88. INT. PALMERO OFFICE MED. SHOT
Rico is still at the table, automatically counting the money. Grouped around the table are Sam, Scabby, Otero, and one or two unnamed gangsters. Sam, his head buried in his hands, is keening, his mumbled words not distinguishable. Now, from outside, the sound of footsteps—someone is running up the stairs. All present glance toward the door.

89. INT. PALMERO OFFICE MED. PAN SHOT
past the group at the table to the door where Bat Carillo is standing. He closes the door. The men tense.

BAT:

Flaherty and two other dicks downstairs, Boss. They're coming up.

Rico whips off his coat and wraps the money in it.

RICO:

Stay there, Otero! (To Sam.) They won't know nothing unless they picked Tony up—give 'em the salve. I'll be right there, listening.

Sam, scared to death, still sits with his head buried in his palms. Rico nudges him viciously.

RICO:

Snap out of it, you!

We PAN to follow him as he runs lightly across the room and slips into the passage behind the secret panel. All others remain in their places. Sam hastily starts spreading his cards on the table as usual.

90. INT. PALMERO OFFICE MED. SHOT
There is a knock on the door. Vettori nods and Carillo opens it. Flaherty and two other dicks step in, right hands in overcoat pockets. Sam waves for Carillo to leave. The bouncer exits. Flaherty walks into CAMERA,

to Sam. The other dicks stay by the door. Sam dreamily plays solitaire without so much as a glance at the flat-foot.

91. INT. PALMERO OFFICE CLOSE SHOT
on Sam, Flaherty, and Otero. Flaherty hasn't a thing on this gang and is only fishing for information, but he is tough.

FLAHERTY:

Happy New Year, boys! There's a lonesome touring car down the street. Do you know anything about it?[20]

Sam effectively conceals his inward fears, laughs, and shakes his head. From this question he knows Flaherty is not hot on the trail.

SAM:

I got a good cafe business. I don't know nothing about automobiles what's been left.

FLAHERTY:

You might know if some of the smart young guys who hang around here had anything to do with it, wouldn't you?

Sam shakes his head. Otero then asks a leading question.

OTERO:

Wasn't anybody in it?

FLAHERTY:

Yeah, one guy—but not when we got there. He beat it—we got a good description of him, though!

92. INT. PALMERO OFFICE MED. CLOSE-UP RICO
in the passageway. He is sitting cross-legged on the floor with his head against the door, listening to the conversation. A flashlight is trained on the money in

piles on his coat on the floor. In the center of it is his automatic—ready. He keeps on counting. His face is harsh.[21]

93. INT. PALMERO OFFICE MED. CLOSE SHOT
on the group in the office. Vettori speaks convincingly:

SAM:
I keep telling you—I don't know nothing about it!

Flaherty stares hard at him for a long moment, then his glance flicks around the room. There is nothing suspicious here. He turns to the door, addressing the other dicks:

FLAHERTY:
Let's get going. As long as Vettori doesn't know anything about it.

The other two detectives step outside. Flaherty pauses in the doorway.

FLAHERTY:
Oh, say . . . you heard the news, Vettori?

Sam silently looks his question.

FLAHERTY:
Somebody got Alvin McClure over at the Bronze Peacock.

SAM:
McClure! That's terrible. Some guys are sure careless with the lead. What a tough break for Arnie!

94. INT. PALMERO OFFICE MED. CLOSE-UP

FLAHERTY (grimly):
It's going to be a tough break for a lot of birds! Well, so long . . . I forgot to wish you fellows a Merry Christmas!

He closes the door.

95. INT. PALMERO OFFICE MED. FULL SHOT
Sam walks over, shoots the bolt on the door, and peeps through the little lookout window. Rico comes out of his hiding place and spreads his coat and the money on the table. Sam joins him. Both men show the effects of the strain. Otero is unmoved; Scabby and the others come nearer.

96. INT. PALMERO OFFICE CLOSE SHOT
Sam drops into a chair, nerves frayed.

SAM:

It's Tony . . . I can't get 'im . . . The kid's a great driver . . . must o' lost his nerve . . . (Sighs heavily. Shakes his head. Then, wearily.) Well, let's see the color of that money . . . (Puts out his hand. But Rico, standing at the other end of the table, suddenly puts a guarding arm over the money, which is lying on the table in stacks.)

RICO:

Not so fast, Sam. I got my own ideas of a split this trip! And you can take it my way or leave it. We ain't beggin' you!

Sam, abandoning his customary lassitude, now jumps up.

SAM:

Yeah? Well, I bossed this job and I get my split the regular way or else . . .

RICO:

How'd you boss this job? By sittin' here in your office drinkin' wine?[22] Well, that don't go no more. Not with me, it don't. We're done. I been takin' orders too long from you!

SAM (an ugly, menacing look on his face):

And you'll keep on takin' orders, too—or you'll get out so fast that . . .

RICO (interrupting him):
Maybe it won't be *me* that gets out . . .

SAM:
Guess the boys got something to say about that!

97. INT. PALMERO OFFICE MED. CLOSE SHOT INCLUDING WHOLE GROUP

as Sam and Rico are standing, they occupy places on the opposite sides of the table. Sam, as he finishes his last sentence, looks challengingly at the gang. But the gang, one by one, slowly move over to Rico's side of the table and silently range themselves behind him. There is not a word spoken. Rico stands, a triumphant half-smile lighting up his face. Sam's face drops; he lets out an involuntary:

SAM:
Oh! That's it, eh?

RICO:
That's it, all right. You've got so you can dish it out, but you can't take it no more. You're through!

Sam's face hardens. He stares at the gang. For a while he doesn't seem able to believe the situation.

RICO:
Well?

SAM (slowly):
The splits okay with me, Rico!

RICO (turning to gangsters behind him):
How about you, boys?

Otero, Scabby, and Bat reply simultaneously:

THE GANG:
It's okay with us, *Boss!*

98. INT. PALMERO OFFICE CLOSE SHOT SAM AND RICO

Rico steps up to Sam and says:

RICO:

No hard feelings, eh, Sam? We gotta stick together. There's a rope around my neck right now and they only hang you once. If anybody gets yellow and squeals—*my gun's gonna speak its piece.*[23]

SAM:

No—no hard feelin's. If this is good with the boys, it's good with me!

Otero sticks his head into the picture, addresses Rico.

OTERO:

Can I go see my woman now, Boss?

RICO (with an indulgent wave of his hand):

Sure! Now don't spend all your money on her, Otero. You worked hard for it . . .

An appreciative laugh from the unseen gang rewards this, as we

FADE OUT

SEVENTH SEQUENCE

FADE IN

99. INT. MA MAGDALENA'S FRUIT STORE FULL SHOT NIGHT

Ma Magdalena is an old, fat, ugly Sicilian hag. She is a notorious fence and the confidante of half of Little Italy. For a blind she runs a small basement fruit store, behind which are her office and living quarters. She is sitting in the rear of her shallow shop and as we fade in we hear:

NEWSBOY:

Extra! Extra! Crime Commissioner shot!

A newsboy crosses the store to Ma and sells her a paper. As he goes away, Rico enters and passes the boy who exits, slamming the door behind him. Ma Magdalena takes one look at Rico's set face, rises, and motions him into the back room. She hobbles after, on her stick. The newspaper is still in her hand. (This is all silent; only by a surreptitious motion of his hand does Rico beckon to Ma to follow him.)

100. INT. MA MAGDALENA'S OFFICE CLOSE SHOT

One wall of the small room Ma Magdalena uses as an office is lined with shelves of canned goods. There is a makeshift desklike affair and litter of odds and ends.

MA (perching on chair at desk, throwing down her newspaper, she looks inquiringly at Rico):

Well, Rico, business good?

Rico pulls out his split, peels off a few bills which he returns to his pocket, and hands the bulk of the money to the old woman. During this, Rico is smiling.

RICO:

Can't complain. Here . . . salt this away with the rest.

MA (while deftly counting the money):

Had a big New Year's Eve, did you?

RICO (with satisfied expression):

Plenty big.

MA (having finished counting, she looks up):

Twenty-seven hundred.

RICO (nods):

That's right. How much have I got now, all told?

MA (looking ceilingward, her face screwed up as she figures, counting on her fingers):

Lemme see . . . 'Twas thirty-one hundred—then the two grand you gave me a week ago—and now this pile . . . (looks at Rico.) Seven thous' eight hundred.

RICO:

Good enough. Hang onto it good, Magdalena. Never know when I'm gonna need it. There'll be lots o' fun, startin' tomorrow.

MA (shrugging):

Good, you know what to do if things get too hot . . .

RICO:

The hideout all fixed up?

MA:

Look at it yourself . . .

101. CLOSE SHOT HIDEOUT

Through this shot we hear Ma's voice:

MA:

Best hideout in the world . . . Nobody find you here . . . !

This is a shot of the tiny cubbyhole hideout, a very narrow room, not much larger than a closet. It contains a cot and chair.

102. CLOSE SHOT OFFICE

Rico nods. It is a swell hideout. Ma swings the shelves back in place and moves to Rico. Tapping him on the shoulder with her stick, she asks:

MA (wheedling):

Look, Rico, ain't you got a nice little girl who wants a big diamond?

RICO (scornfully):

Me buy a diamond for a Jane from a fence?

MA:

You are cold, Rico. Don't care for anything except yourself—your hair and your gun.

Ma shakes her head and makes a clucking noise. This man is not human.

RICO (smiling):

I might like a diamond for myself—like big shots wear . . .

The old hag's face lights with avarice.

RICO (concludes):

One o' these days. Maybe soon . . . (Now Rico notices newspaper on Ma's desk; with a nod indicates it.) Here, lemme see that . . .

Ma, with a knowing, crooked smile, hands him the paper. We can see the large display-type headline emblazoned across the front page. Rico takes up the paper, starts reading it with interest.

INSERT Thugs Kill Crime Commissioner in Nightclub Holdup

Rico grunts. We see his hands folding the paper so as to be able to read the story properly.

INSERT A SECOND OF THE NEWSPAPER

The thug who shot Alvin McClure was
described by one eye-witness as a small,
unhealthy-looking foreigner.

103. MA MAGDALENA'S OFFICE CLOSE-UP RICO

His face shows annoyance.

RICO:

Where do they get that unhealthy stuff? I never been sick a day in my life. (Irritated, he crumples the newspaper and throws it on the floor.)

FADE OUT

EIGHTH SEQUENCE

FADE IN

104. TONY'S FLAT EARLY MORNING MED. SHOT

This is a combination living and bedroom in one of those wretched tenement houses that are typical Little Italy. The apartment itself perhaps consists of a bedroom and a kitchen in addition to his room, but we do not see the other chambers at this time.

Tony's bed is made up on a pulled-out davenport. As we fade in, he is lying on it, fully dressed. It is early morning. A feeble city sun sends its rays through the cracks of the room.

105. TONY'S FLAT CLOSE SHOT

Tony, lying on the bed. He is asleep, but a nightmare seems to be torturing him. His face moves convulsively and he tosses about, occasionally throwing his entire body into the air.

Now, suddenly with a shriek, his eyes open, instant terror takes possession of his face, and he jerks himself upright on the bed. Crouched against the wall, he sits there, his eyes darting back and forth as though looking for hidden enemies. Then, satisfied that he is alone, he seems to quiet down a bit; with the back of palm, he wipes away the perspiration that has gathered on his forehead. Then with trembling hands, he searches his pocket for cigarettes. Finding the crumpled package, he pulls out a weed and with unsteady hands lights it. But after a puff or two, he leaps up from the bed.

106. TONY'S FLAT MED. SHOT

Tony, nervously moving the cigarette between his lips, is walking up and down the tiny room. Now, unable to stand the torture of his thoughts any longer, he jerks the cigarette out of his mouth and throws it on the floor, viciously crushing it under his heel.

TONY (almost shrieking the words):
Oh, God! I can't stand it . . . I can't . . .

The door now opens quietly and Mrs. Passa, an old Italian woman with a parchmentlike yellowed face, comes in. She is fully dressed for the street.

MRS. PASSA (coming forward, with a look of concern):
What's matter, Antonio? Why you no sleep?

Tony comes to a halt, stares at his mother. Mrs. Passa continues:

MRS. PASSA:
You sick, maybe?

TONY:
Yes . . . no . . . I don't know . . . (Bursting out irritably.) Can't a guy get up when he wants without having to answer a lot of fool questions . . . ?

MRS. PASSA (slowly nodding her head through this speech):
You stay out late, Tony? You drink lotta wine?

TONY (turning away):
Oh! Lemme alone . . .

Mrs. Passa looks sadly at the boy as his back is turned. Then she says:

MRS. PASSA:
Listen, Antonio, I leave spaghetti on stove. Yes? When you feel better, eat some, eh? Do you good.

She starts toward door again. At this Tony wheels around and asks frantically:

TONY:
Where you going, Ma?

MRS. PASSA (spreading her hands):
I go to work.

TONY (hanging on desperately):
It's early yet . . . You don't have to go . . .

MRS. PASSA:
I got to go see Mrs. Mangia . . . she has new baby. Only think! That will be six.

TONY (with a sickly smile):
One is too much . . . a bad egg like me is . . .

MRS. PASSA (a softer look coming into her eyes):
You ain't a bad egg, Antonio. You are only lazy. You go with bad boys . . . (Stepping closer; her tone full of reminiscent tenderness.) You was good boy, Antonio . . . You remember when you sing in choir with Father McNeil . . . You in white, remember?

Tony's face suddenly becomes rigid. His eyes stare off into the distance. He whispers:

TONY:
Father McNeil . . .

MRS. PASSA:
The church was beautiful . . . you little boy with long hair . . . the big candles . . . flowers . . . remember, Antonio?

The verbal picture has a terrific effect on Tony. Inner sobs shake him. His lips twitch, he grasps his mother's arm as he says, almost hysterically:

TONY:
Don't go away, Ma . . . I don't want you to go away . . . don't leave me . . .

MRS. PASSA:
Antonio! (Her hand goes out to caress his hair.) No, no . . . I stay . . . I no go to work . . . I . . .

But Tony cannot bear her touch. He shrinks away, his voice is harsh again as he snaps:

TONY:

Oh, go right ahead, go! I'm all right—sure I'm all right . . . .

Mrs. Passa, repulsed, lets her hand drop. She sighs, then slowly, without a word, she turns and goes to door. At the door she turns back and looks at her son as though expecting his summons again. But Tony is silent, again he is fumbling for a cigarette, which now he sticks into his mouth without lighting. Mrs. Passa goes out.

107. TONY'S FLAT CLOSE-UP TONY
He whispers:

TONY:

Father McNeil . . .

DISSOLVE IN ON:

108. EXT. STREET NEAR ROMAN CATHOLIC CHURCH DUSK SNOWING LONG SHOT
A deserted stretch of street.[24] For a while no one is seen in the picture. Then a solitary figure slowly walks into it, headed down the street. This is Tony.

109. EXT. STREET CLOSE-UP TONY
His head is still lifted as he stares hard ahead of him, as though seeking encouragement. Now he nods, twice to himself. He has now reached a decision, starts forward.

110. EXT. STREET MEDIUM SHOT
Now Otero lurches into the scene. Otero is patently drunk; he is almost reeling as he hails the boy with a jubilant:

OTERO (at the top of his voice):

Hey, Tony!

Tony stops, notices Otero. His figure seems to shrink and he draws his head between his shoulders, looking out of scared eyes at the Mexican. Otero lurches up to him, slapping him on the shoulder with a great show of friendliness.

111. EXT. STREET CLOSE SHOT

OTERO:

Ha! Where you been? I look all over . . . Rico—he say come and get your split.

Tony shakes his head. He is unable to utter words.

OTERO (staring at him):

What's matter, Tony? You don't want split, huh? You craz'?

TONY (softly):

I ain't crazy, Otero, but I don't want no split.

OTERO:

Listen, Tony . . . Rico know you lose your nerve. Be a man, Rico say. That is good. Be a man. You no better be yellow.

The words seem to strike Tony with especial force. He starts biting his lips, wringing his hands in silent agony. Otero laughs. Again he slaps the boy on the shoulder.

OTERO:

Look at me! I am Ramon Otero, a great brave man. I ain't afraid nobody or nothing. And Rico—he my friend. I love him with a great love. I, Ramon Otero, love Rico with great big love.[25]

During the main part of the speech Tony remains silent. But before the Mexican has finished his oration, Tony turns and starts walking away.

112. EXT. ROMAN CATHOLIC CHURCH MEDIUM SHOT

Having come to the end of his harangue, the Mexican notices that Tony has left him. Now he hurries after the other.

OTERO (catching up to Tony):

Hey, Tony, where you go, huh?

TONY:

To church.[26]

OTERO (alarmed):

Church . . . you mean . . . go . . . confess?

Tony nods assent and continues toward the church. Drunk as he is, Otero realizes what the other is doing and is stunned by the discovery.

OTERO (shooting out his hand after Tony as though to stop him):

Hey, Tony, you mustn't . . . Tony, please, not talk to the priest . . . (But Tony is rapidly walking away.)

OTERO (crying out in alarm):

Tony . . . Tony . . . no tell nothing to nobody . . . Tony, please.

Tony quickens his pace and hurries away from Otero.

DISSOLVE INTO:

113. INT. PALERMO OFFICE MED. CLOSE SHOT

Rico, Sam, and Scabby are in the room, also Bat Carillo, when Otero bursts in. The excitement seems to have sobered Otero and he is quite coherent as he rushes up to Rico and tells him the news:

OTERO (gasping with excitement):

I found Tony . . . but it's too late. He's craz', craz'. I tell 'im, be a man . . . but he just shake his head and go to the priest . . .

Shocked by this intelligence, the gangsters look at each other. They are all aghast. Only Rico nods knowingly as though he had expected this.

SAM (gasping):

The priest?!

RICO:

Well, I guess that's it. What'd you expect of a guy that's been a choir boy . . . ? We ain't got any time to waste.

SAM:

It's only the priest! Confession—that's all!

RICO:

Yeah, I know. I'm as religious as you are any day. But a guy who'll talk to the priest will talk to other people, too. Get yourself a car, Sam, and let's go.[27]

SAM (suddenly putting a palm over his face with an expression of horror; whispering):

Not me! Take . . . take Scabby . . .

RICO (impatiently):

Scabby's no good!

SCABBY (a look of relief spreading over his face):

No, I'm no good!

RICO (now looking hard at Otero):

Can you drive, Otero?

Otero hesitates a moment, looks at Rico as though he were also about to refuse, then nods:

OTERO:

Yes . . .

RICO:

All right, there's no other way out . . . We'll use the black roadster . . . (Quickly dashes for the door, Otero following him.)

DISSOLVE INTO:

114. EXT. CHURCH DUSK SNOWING LONG SHOT

It is still dusk. The snow falls faster now. A black roadster, hugging the curb, approaches and slows down near the church.

115. EXT. CHURCH ROADSTER MED. CLOSE-UP
Otero and Rico are peering through the windshield. The car is barely crawling. Otero points. Rico's face becomes as grim as death. He lifts the big automatic which has been resting on his knee.

116. EXT. CHURCH MED. LONG SHOT
Tony appears on sidewalk and starts walking up church steps. Then Rico's voice is heard:

RICO (out of scene):
Tony!

The boy whips around. There is a fusillade of shots. Tony falls without a sound. The gears of a car scream; the exhaust roars. (We see nothing of the car or Rico during this scene.)

FADE OUT

NINTH SEQUENCE

FADE IN

117. EXT. STREET LONG SHOT DAY
As we fade in, a typical Italian procession is slowly moving down the street. In the van is an Italian band—confined to brasses—playing a slow, mournful funeral march. Following this, the hearse, richly laden with flowers, wreaths, floral blankets, inscribed ribbons, etc. Behind the hearse, a number of closed automobiles—limousines, of the kind furnished by undertakers for such processions.
NOTE: Horses with plumes, etc. would undoubtedly be more picturesque and quite in character for the funeral. But, should it be found more desirable to use automobiles, the atmosphere can still be maintained by the employment of the latter. This script assumes that motor vehicles will be used throughout the scene.[28]

118. EXT. STREET MED. SHOT
The funeral procession from another angle. A few of the

motor cars are included and a section of the hearse. Now the legends on the ribbons are more clearly distinguishable and bear the routine inscriptions: Rest in Peace, Gates Ajar, etc. If desired, individual names can also be featured on the ribbons: Sam Vettori, Ramon Otero, Mother, St. Mary's Young Men's Club, Alumni Association, P.S. 25, etc.

Throughout this, of course, the funeral march goes on.

119. INT. MRS. PASSA'S AUTOMOBILE CLOSE SHOT

This is a closed car, driven by a uniformed chauffeur. In the back seat is Mrs. Passa, Tony's mother. Next to her is old Ma Magdalena. Both women are dressed in black. Mrs. Passa is sobbing aloud.

MRS. PASSA (between her sobs):

Tony . . . Tony . . . Why you go away like this, why you leave me . . . ?

MA (taking hold of her arm, softly):

Ssh! No cry, Mrs. Passa . . . please . . . you no can help . . .

MRS. PASSA (keening):

Why I not die? First my husband . . . then the baby . . . now Antonio, he go too! Why I raise them? Why I see them grow? . . Tony, he didn't hurt nobody . . . He was good . . . Why? Why?

CUT TO:

120. INT. A SIMILAR LIMOUSINE CLOSE SHOT

In this are seated Killer Pepi, Bat Carillo, and Sam.

SAM:

We're gonna plant the kid right. That'll look good.

BAT:

See all them flowers . . . ! That hearse is sure decked out pretty . . .

SAM:

Well, this wasn't no time to be tight with money. Tony deserved a swell send-off. Poor kid!

PEPI:

But Rico's wreath beat them all. Big like this . . . (Spreads his hands to illustrate.) And all it said on it was "Tony," not even Rico's name.

BAT:

Yeah, Rico's no piker.

SAM:

Tony looks like he was asleep . . . don't look a bit changed . . .

BAT:

Beats me how they do it.

CUT TO:

121. INT. TAXICAB CLOSE SHOT

The cab is parked on a side street, unnoticed. In the back seat are Joe and Olga. Joe's face is white, drawn. He is nervously puffing at a cigarette, fingering it feverishly from time to time. Olga holds onto his left arm with both her hands.

JOE (suddenly flinging the cigarette out of the window, he starts hammering his knee with a nervous, impotent rage):

What'd they have to do it for? Why couldn't they let him alone? Who'd he ever harm? Oh, the dirty . . .

OLGA (still holding on to his arm, now drawing closer to him):

We shouldn't have come, Joey. I begged you not to come. You're getting excited and its all for nothing . . . *You* can't help poor Tony anymore!

JOE:

I had to come. I had to see them taking him away . . . (Now raising his voice to a tragic pitch.) They forced him into that job . . . He was scared. He didn't want to go . . . (With a final bitter outburst.) Like me. Tony was like me. I didn't want to go neither . . . they forced me . . .

OLGA:

That was your last job, Joey. We'll go away . . . I told you we'll go away. We can get bookings all over the country . . .

JOE (his face drawn in fear):

But they'll get me. You watch and see. Once in a gang, always in a gang. They'll get me the way they got Tony . . .

OLGA (sternly):

No! I can save you. I'm *going* to take you away!

JOE (suddenly breaking down):

Yes! Let's try . . . I can never look them in the face again. Not after this . . . I'll do anything . . . (Very eagerly; a cunning quality coming into his voice.) We won't go right away, though, Olga. That would give it away . . . I'll just lie low first . . . keep on dancing at the club . . . and stay away from Rico. Then when the coast is clear, you and me beat it . . .

Olga, her face beaming with happiness, strokes his arm tenderly.

CUT TO:

122. INT. RICO'S CAR CLOSE SHOT

Here we discover Rico and Otero seated in the back seat. For a second or two they are silent. Then Otero says:

OTERO:

Just the same, it's hard on his old lady . . .

RICO:

Well, it's Tony's own fault. I didn't want to do it, did I?

OTERO:

No, you had to do it, Boss.

RICO (nodding):

I had to do it. When you're in this racket you gotta take your chances. Tony was a good kid, but he was weak. There's no room for that kind. It was to be us or him—so it had to be *him!* This is a tough game—you gotta know how to take it and how to give it!

OTERO (suddenly pointing to sidewalk through window):

Look, Rico, there's Flaherty, the bull!

CUT TO:

123. EXT. STREET MED. CLOSE SHOT
Standing on the sidewalk is Flaherty. He is in plain clothes. With hands stuck in his pockets, he is studying the funeral procession as it goes past him. In background idle spectators, loiterers, passers-by.

124. EXT. STREET MED. SHOT
This is shot from Flaherty's angle: he is with his back to the camera. As Rico's car passes, Flaherty—now showing his face somewhat in profile so as to establish his expression—smiles ironically and waves his hand with mocking, elaborate courtesy.[29]

125. INT. RICO'S LIMOUSINE CLOSE SHOT
Rico, bent to the window, sees Flaherty and perfunctorily waves back, somewhat irritated.

OTERO:

Things must be gettin' pretty hot, Boss. What's he want?

RICO (shrugs):

Aw, he's just stallin'. Hasn't got a thing on me . . .[30]

They sit in silence for a while. Now, a long piercing scream can be heard from the outside, instantly followed by drawn-out crying. Rico looks out of narrowed eyes; Otero shivers, crosses himself.

OTERO:

Tony's old lady . . . she sure is taking it hard.

RICO (with a look of disgust on his face):

That's a woman for you.

Otero's face becomes mild for a moment. Then in an apologetic soft voice, he says:

OTERO:

Well . . . Tony was her son . . .

Rico raises his eyebrows with an expression equivalent to a shrug, then pulls out his watch and looks at it.

RICO:

Gee, we're movin' slow.

OTERO:

We got plenty o' time. That banquet don't start till eight.

RICO (nods; now relaxes and settles back in his seat; then):

Too bad Tony won't be there . . .

Otero nods.

FADE OUT

TENTH SEQUENCE

FADE IN

126. INSERT ELECTRIC SIGN

C L U B
P
A
L
E
R
M
O
DANCING

DISSOLVE THROUGH THIS SIGN TO:

127. INT. CLUB PALERMO BANQUET ROOM CLOSE-UP

A man's hand, about to open a program. Just now his thumb is resting on the cover; the owner of the hand seems to be studying it. (The hand is Rico's. It is important at this juncture that he should be wearing a ring either exactly resembling or similar to the ring worn by Pete Montana in Arnie's office in scene 24.)

The program that Rico is studying is a semistiff cardboard affair, with two embossed angels holding an equally embossed shield in midair.[31] Printed on the shield:

TESTIMONIAL BANQUET
FOR
MR. CAESAR ENRICO BANDELLO
GIVEN BY
THE PALERMO BOYS

Dangling from the shield are two entwined ribbons, embossed, and the legend:

"FRIENDSHIP—LOYALTY"

Below the shield, between the ribbons, are two turtle doves, cooing. The whole cover has a rich frosting of golds, silvers, reds, and blues.

Now the hand slowly turns the page, disclosing the advertising section. This is divided into a half- and two quarter-page advertisements. In the upper half we find printed:

COMPLIMENTS TO A TRUE PAL
MR. C. BANDELLO
FROM A TRUE PAL
MR. SAM VETTORI

In the left quarter:

TO RICO:
REMEMBER THE RIVER
REMEMBER THE BROOK
REMEMBER THE FRIEND
WHO ADVERTISED IN THIS BOOK.
(Signed) BAT CARILLO

In the righthand quarter:

COMPLIMENTS OF
JOE SANSONE (K.O.)
"Lightweight King of Little Italy"
and
HIS LADY FRIEND
MISS ANGELINA VECCHIONI

The hand turns to the next page. This section is divided into three ads, each one taking up one third of the page. The uppermost one says:

"BE A SPORT—DRESS TO KILL"
DRESS SUITS FOR HIRE
Tuxedos used at this banquet
exclusively rented by us.
COMPLIMENTS TO MR. BANDELLO AND
THE PALERMO BOYS
PARIS • ROME STYLE OUTFITTERS
642 Fairmond Avenue

And in the ad below this:

"THE HELPING HAND"
UNCLE'S
That's all.

The third ad, occupying the bottom space:

"Ma Magdalena"
FRESH FRUITS AND VEGETABLES
TO RICO
A GOOD MAN HARD TO FIND!

Now as the hand turns the page again, CAMERA PANS UP so as to include Rico's face. Rico is dressed in a tuxedo—obviously hired and while not grotesquely ill-fitting the suit is by no means a perfect fit.

RICO:

It certainly is a swell-lookin' battin' order! That Scabby is a clever guy to get it up so good-lookin' with gold on it an' everythin' . . .

SAM:

It cost all the boys plenty money.

(Both during this speech and during the inserts, we hear conversation, shouts, laughter from the unseen guests.)

128. AT TABLE

Now the CAMERA TRUCKS BACK, disclosing the banquet table in all its magnificence.

129. INT. CLUB PALERMO BANQUET ROOM TRUCK SHOT

As the CAMERA TRUCKS BACK, we see the various guests seated on both sides of the long table. (If it is possible to photograph this with the camera running on a track above the table, the progress should be down the length of the festive board. Otherwise the best plan may be to arrange a horseshoe table, with guests ranged on one side only, CAMERA FACING THEM. In the latter case, the space enclosed by the horseshoe should be left clear for action.)

All the members of the gang are present: Rico seated in the place of honor either at the head of the table or at the center of the horseshoe; on his left the Big Boy, on Rico's right Sam Vettori; then Otero, Scabby, Killer Pepi, Bat Carillo, Kid Bean, Ottavio Vettori, Blackie Avezzano, etc. (Joe Sansone is an ex-lightweight, slender, small, with cauliflower ears; Ottavio Vettori, Sam's cousin, a husky Americanized Italian about twenty-one; Kid Bean is a Sicilian, dark as a Negro. The others, unless already established, the usual gangster type.)

Every other seat is occupied by the ladies of the gang. Cheap, semiprostitute, blondined, overdressed types. There are, however, no women around Rico. Dangling from the chandeliers are red, green, and white streamers. On the wall above Rico's head is an orange and blue square banner, very much like a college varsity affair, inscribed with the simple legend Club Palermo, accompanied by an equally gigantic monogram embodying the two letters.

130. INT. CLUB PALERMO BANQUET ROOM GENERAL SHOT

The gang and their ladies are busily eating. In the course of this, there are various rough pranks played: rolls and occasionally salt cellars and spoons and knives thrown around; a handspring on the top of a chair by one of the younger members of the gang; an amorous scene between a lady and her boyfriend, etc. The din is terrific. Ad lib conversation.

131. INT. CLUB PALERMO BANQUET ROOM CLOSE SHOT HEAD OF TABLE

Sam Vettori rises and, banging the table, raps for silence. When comparative quiet prevails, he shouts at the top of his voice:

SAM:

What the Sam Hill! Ain't this a fine way to act at a banquet? What do you think you are—a couple gashouse yaps? Cut the chatter. Scabby's gonna make a speech.

132. A SECTION OF THE TABLE MED. CLOSE SHOT

OTTAVIO (making a noise like a goat):
Baa! Baa!

A GIRL (sitting next to him):
Gosh! Ain't that cute!

PEPI:
Oh, that ain't nothin'. (Putting three fingers in his mouth, he blows a tremendous blast.)

OTTAVIO (screaming):
Wow! The cops! Baa! Baa!

CUT BACK TO:

133. HEAD OF TABLE CLOSE-UP
Scabby stands up. He is manifestly ill at ease, embarrassed. He fidgets a long time before launching into his speech:

SCABBY:
Well, fellows, you all know what we're here for, so what's the good of me tellin' you all 'bout it? Rico is a great guy an' . . . Well, gee whiz, Rico, I don't know how to talk fancy but— (pulls a platinum and diamond watch out of his pocket, awkwardly dangling it on its chain) this here is for you, see? From the boys!

INSERT DIAMOND AND PLATINUM WATCH WITH THE INSCRIPTION

TO OUR STANDARD BEARER AND LEADER
FROM THE PALERMO BOYS

A VOICE (coming over the screen):
Come on! Everybody clap like . . .

134. GENERAL SHOT BANQUET HALL
Bedlam has broken loose. Chairs are overturned, napkins waved, plates crashed against the table. The

women scream; the men cheer wildly. Ottavio jumps up on his chair, and, acting like a college cheerleader, gives the signal.

OTTAVIO:

What do you say, boys? Three cheers for Rico!

Led by Ottavio, comes a regular college cheer: "Rico! Rico! Rico!" Catcalls, whistling, applause, etc.[32]

135. CLOSE SHOT RICO

His face is beaming with pride as he stands up and waves for silence.

RICO:

All right, if you birds want me to make a speech, here you are! I want to thank you guys for this banquet. It sure is swell. The liquor is good so they tell me, I don't drink it myself, and the food don't leave nothing to be desired. I guess we all had a swell time and it sure is good to see all you guys gathered together.[33] Well, I guess that's about all. Only I wish you guys wouldn't get drunk and raise Cain, as that's the way a lot of birds get bumped off.

Rico sits down. Prolonged applause. Now Scabby runs up behind Rico's back and, bending close to him, says:

SCABBY:

A couple newspaper guys, Boss. They wanta take a flashlight. It's for the Sunday section of the paper.

RICO (indulgently but obviously pleased):

All right, Let 'em come! They'll have to make it snappy . . .[34] (Pulls out his comb and starts combing his hair.)

136. FULL SHOT

The photographer and the flashlight man take up their positions in the foreground. Farther back, the gangsters sit up, posing for all they're worth. There is a general fixing of ties, hasty smoothing of hair, etc. The photographer waves, the flashlight goes off, a cloud of smoke through which we hear Ottavio's scream:

OTTAVIO:

Eeeh! I'm shot!

General laughter.

CUT TO:

137. INT. CLUB PALERMO STAIRCASE CLOSE SHOT
We see Flaherty with another dick, coming up the stairs.

CUT BACK TO:

138. INT. CLUB PALERMO BANQUET
Rico is sitting in his place. Sam leans toward him.

BIG BOY:

That was a bad play, Rico, that flashlight. They may pick you up on that.

RICO (shrugs; laughs):

Aw, what do I care? Don't I want people to see what the boys think of me?

SAM (tapping him on the shoulder; looks around as he says this):

But say, where's your pal, that dancer guy, Joe Massara?

Rico's face darkens instantly. His expression shows that the same thought must have been troubling him [all] evening.

RICO:

He didn't come. He hasn't been around for a long time.

SAM (insinuatingly):

He hasn't quit on you, Rico?

RICO (sullenly):

Shut up, Sam. You tend to your business and let me tend to mine.[35]

CUT TO:

139. INT. CLUB PALERMO BANQUET ROOM CLOSE SHOT

Flaherty and the other cop come into the room. Flaherty stands at the doorframe, folds his arms on his chest, and looks into the room.

CUT BACK TO:

140. CLOSE-UP RICO

Rico turns to Big Boy.

RICO:

What does that bull want here? I'll show him where he gets off. (Angrily rises, pushes back his chair, and starts off.)

BIG BOY:

Careful, Rico!

CUT TO:

141. INT. CLUB PALERMO CLOSE SHOT

Flaherty still at the door. Now in a low voice, he exchanges a few words with the other cop. They both smile. Now Rico stalks into the picture.

RICO (brusquely):

Well, who invited you here?

Flaherty looks over Rico's new finery with deliberate insolence. Then:

FLAHERTY:

Getting up in the world, aren't you, Rico?

RICO (feet planted wide apart):

What's that to you?

FLAHERTY (still pleasantly):

Gosh, nothing. I'm glad to see you decked out like

this. You see, I got my eye on you, Rico. Don't forget that I'm your friend. I like to see a young fellow getting up in the world. Well, so long!

RICO:

Fall down the steps, will you?

FLAHERTY (still pleasantly):

Thanks! (Turns to go. Then, as he reaches the door, he turns back to Rico.) Say, somebody threw a brick in Meyerblum's window last night . . . You don't happen to know anything about a platinum and diamond watch that was stolen, do you? In case you hear about it, let me know . . .

Rico, taken aback, is really at a loss for an answer. Flaherty turns again, goes through the door. Rico continues to stare after him.

FADE OUT

ELEVENTH SEQUENCE

FADE IN

INSERT A NEWSPAPER PICTURE

reproducing the flashlight photograph taken at the banquet in the previous sequence. Caption under the picture:

"Little Caesar" Bandello Given
Testimonial by Followers

Through this:

DISSOLVE INTO:

142. INT. BRONZE PEACOCK LOBBY MED CLOSE SHOT

Little Arnie and DeVoss present in the lobby. Little Arnie is comfortably seated in an armchair near the telephone booth, smoking a heavy black cigar. DeVoss is standing before him, hands in pockets, a worried expression on his face. In Arnie's hand we see the newspaper carrying the flashlight photograph. Now he throws it on the floor, annoyed and disgusted.

ARNIE:

A banquet, huh? Rico got far . . . too far! So now he's got to stop . . . I'm saying he's got to stop . . .

DeVOSS:

Oh, Arnie, are you fellows going to start another scrap? What's the use of my paying heavy money to you for protection if there's never any peace?

ARNIE:

Don't you worry, DeVoss. There'll be peace soon enough. I'm saying Rico's got to stop—so he's gonna stop, see! He's been nosin' in on my territory and that's all wet with me.

143. INT. BRONZE PEACOCK LOBBY CLOSE SHOT JOE

Joe is standing on the other side of the telephone booth, which effectively conceals him from Arnie and DeVoss. He is listening to their conversation with rapt attention.

CUT BACK TO:

144. INT. BRONZE PEACOCK LOBBY CLOSE SHOT

Little Arnie bends forward and says menacingly, emphasizing his remarks with an extended forefinger:

ARNIE:

I'm sittin' here, see? I'm sittin' here quiet, smokin' a cigar, see? But a coupla my boys ain't sittin' here . . . They're out lookin' for Rico. And they got their gats with 'em, too. Catch on? And once they find 'im, it won't be no banquet Rico gets—it'll be a wake!

DeVOSS (shaking his head):

Well, Arnie, you know best. I never met Rico.[36] I don't know what he looks like . . . but I do want a little less excitement around here for a change . . .

Arnie rises, laughs:

ARNIE:

There won't be no excitement, after today . . .

He and DeVoss start walking off.

145. INT. BRONZE PEACOCK LOBBY MED. SHOT

We see the two men crossing the lobby, toward DeVoss's office. They disappear into the office. Joe Massara, from behind the telephone booth, is watching them closely. Now, as the door closes behind the two men, Joe rushes into the telephone booth and hastily drops a nickel into the slot. We hear the coin ringing the bell.

It is at this moment that Olga enters the lobby. As she is only a few steps away from the booth, she hears the bell and glances at the telephone booth. When she sees Joe, she comes to a halt.

JOE (in the booth):

Phelps 2284 . . .

As Olga hears the voice and the number she picks up her head in astonishment. Her face darkens and she hurries toward the booth.

146. INT. TELEPHONE BOOTH AT BRONZE PEACOCK CLOSE SHOT

Joe is clicking the receiver now. Apparently he is having trouble obtaining his connection.

147. INT. BRONZE PEACOCK CLOSE-UP JOE IN TELEPHONE BOOTH

JOE (quickly, forcefully):

Otero! This is Joe Massara. I just got a straight tip. Look out for Rico. Little Arnie's after him.

148. INT. CLUB PALERMO CASHIER'S DESK MED. CLOSE SHOT

We see Otero staring stupidly at the hand telephone for an instant. Now he drops it on the floor and turns excitedly to Bat Carillo, who is standing beside him.

OTERO (out of breath):
Where's Rico?

BAT:
Got me! He ain't showed up yet!

OTERO:
Come on, we gotta find him!

They exit on the jump. A waiter comes into the scene and retrieves the telephone.

149. EXT. CLUB PALERMO LONG SHOT
A large touring car with closed curtains is driving slowly past the Club Palermo. There is little movement in the street. Behind the car rattles a big white milk wagon.

150. EXT. CORNER NEWSSTAND MED. CLOSE SHOT
Rico is at the corner newsstand, picking up about ten copies of the same paper. The young kid who is in charge of the stand looks at him in surprise.

NEWSPAPER VENDOR:
Gee, you takin' all them papers, Mr. Rico?

RICO (smiling proudly):
Sure—ten! Ain't I got my pitcher in 'em?

151. EXT. STORE WINDOW CLOSE SHOT
Rico enters and pauses in the lighted display window to look at his watch. It glistens in the light. He regards it proudly. Replacing it, he buttons his coat and takes two or three steps. Then he sees a touring car coming toward him, becomes suspicious, and stops. Suddenly he darts into the doorway and stands there, reaching for his gun.

152. EXT. STORE WINDOW MED. SHOT
The touring car comes closer, slows down. In it are two

women. The car doesn't stop, but slowly continues, hugging the curb. It passes on. Behind it, at some distance, comes a milk wagon.

153. EXT. STORE WINDOW CLOSE SHOT
Rico lifts his eyebrows in surprise and relief as he looks after the car. His face is turned after the touring car as he steps out from behind his shelter.

RICO (to himself):
Well, that's one on me . . .

154. EXT. STREET NEAR CLUB PALERMO MILK WAGON CLOSE SHOT
In the wagon are two Detroit gunmen. Ritz Colonna, Little Arnie's bodyguard, is driving. As he sees Rico he points and yells to the others:

RITZ:
There he is—in front of that store . . .

He slaps his feet on the accelerator and the motor roars.

155. EXT. STREET NEAR CLUB PALERMO MED. LONG SHOT
Knowing, too late, what is coming, Rico wheels around, all the time tugging vainly at his gun. It sticks. The milk wagon drones into high speed. Arnie's men open up. Three streams of fire shoot from the wagon as it sails past. Rico is hit and falls. Above the sound of the shots is the crashing of glass as the machine guns plow into the windows. The thugs are shooting too high in their eagerness. (Might use shot of window being smashed.)

156. EXT. CLUB PALERMO MED. LONG SHOT
A regular knot of men boils out of the Club Palermo: Bat, Otero, Pepi, Kid Bean, and others, all with drawn guns. Curious waiters and some of the bolder guests follow them.[37]

157. EXT. STORE MED. CLOSE-UP

Rico struggles to his feet, putting one hand to his shoulder where he has been wounded. A twisted grin appears; he yells mockingly after the vanished assailants.

RICO:

Fine shots you are!

(The sidewalk is littered with fragments of plate glass from the windows.)

158. EXT. STREET LONG SHOT

From a parallel shooting down on Rico as he is surrounded by his men. A crowd collects from every direction. The core of it progresses slowly toward the Palermo. From the opposite direction Flaherty, the second detective, and a huge policeman push their way to Rico.

159. EXT. STREET NEAR PALERMO MED. CLOSE SHOT

The two detectives and the huge policeman meet Rico and his gang in the crowd. Flaherty grins in a tantalizing fashion. Rico looks at him sourly.

FLAHERTY:

So, somebody finally put one in you?

RICO:

Not enough to hurt.

FLAHERTY:

The old man will be glad to hear it. He takes a lot of interest in you.

RICO:

Tell him the cops couldn't get me no other way so they hired a couple of gunmen.

The crowd laughs at this sally—Rico is a great man, afraid of nothing. The big policeman is writing a report in his notebook.

FLAHERTY (still grinning):

If I hadn't been on the force I'd have taken the job cheap.

RICO:

Listen, Flaherty, did you ever stop to think how you'd look with a lily in your hand?

FLAHERTY:

No, I never did. I been at this game for twenty-five years and I've got better guys than you hung—and I never got a scratch.

RICO:

Don't think you're ever gonna take a ride with me, huh?

FLAHERTY:

When we take a ride together, I'll have the cuffs on you.

RICO:

No buzzard like you'll ever put no cuffs on Rico. Come on, boys!

160. LONG SHOT STREET

Rico and his mob start moving toward entrance of Palermo.

161. CLOSE-UP FLAHERTY

As he stands looking after Rico.

FLAHERTY:

I'll get that swell-headed mug if it's the last thing I ever do.

CUT TO:

162. EXT. STREET NEAR CLUB PALERMO CLOSE SHOT

INT. MILK WAGON

Ritz Colonna, bent over the wheel, is driving furiously. The two other men are behind him.

RITZ:

You saps! Wait till Arnie hears of this . . .

FIRST GANGSTER:

Aw . . . I hit 'im, didn't I?

RITZ:

You couldn't hit a barn door, you hick!

CUT TO:

163. INT. CLUB PALERMO OFFICE CLOSE SHOT
on Rico, who has begun to take off his coat and vest. His arm is beginning to stiffen, and Killer Pepi helps him.

PEPI:

Gee, Boss, I'm sorry. I should o' been with you. You mustn't never go out alone.[38]

Scabby enters with a basin of water and a doctor's kit. He cuts away Rico's shirt and commences to wash the wound. Rico endures this stoically.

164. INT. CLUB PALERMO OFFICE
Otero hurries up to Rico. Rico is standing there, biting his lips, as though in great pain, while Scabby is deftly bandaging his shoulder, binding the arm against the body.

OTERO:

It was Little Arnie, Rico. Joe Massara got the tip and called up. We no could get you in time.

165. INT. CLUB PALERMO OFFICE CLOSE-UP RICO
Rico registers surprise as he hears the name.

RICO:

Oh! Joe, huh? Well, I didn't think he cared enough . . . It was white of him, all right. Maybe I'll go to see him . . . (Lost in thought.) Yeah, I ought to give him a chance to be in on the next job . . .

166. INT. CLUB PALERMO OFFICE MED. CLOSE SHOT
Scabby now has finished the bandaging, and with a last encouraging pat on Rico's shoulder he lets go.

SCABBY:

I didn't study medicine for nothin', did I? If they hadn't got after me and taken away my license . . . (Sighs reminiscently.)

Rico, his wound attended to, again becomes the man of action. He wheels around, facing the gang.

RICO:

I'm going to see Little Arnie tonight! (Pointing to the various characters as he names them.) I want Killer Pepi, Otero, Kid Bean, and Bat to go with me . . .

On this speech we

DISSOLVE INTO:

167. INT. LITTLE ARNIE'S GAMBLING HOUSE CLOSE-UP
of a gun in Killer Pepi's hand shoved hard into the middle of a man's back.

168. CLOSE SHOT
Rico and his men are at the steel door which guards Little Arnie's gambling joint. A fear-paralyzed lookout shrinks away from the automatic which Killer Pepi presses against his body.

PEPI (threatening):

Listen, Handsome. You tell the doorman we're all right or you won't be tellin' nobody nothin' no more.

The man nods dumbly. Rico and his men crowd into the corners so as to be out of sight of the doorman when he looks through the wicket. Otero knocks. The shutter opens. In it appears the familiar face of the doorman.

LOOKOUT (huskily):

These birds are all right.

The door swings open and before the astounded doorman can open his mouth, he is covered by Otero. The others push in after him.

169. GAMBLING HOUSE LOBBY MED. CLOSE SHOT

The doorman has an agonized look. He is sure they are going to kill him for his part in the attack on Rico. Rico, whose arm is bound beneath his coat, speaks to him.

RICO:

Where's Arnie?

The doorman gasps like a fish out of water but no words come. His eyes flick toward the private room. Rico's glance follows his.

RICO:

In the office?

With hands stretched above his head, the doorman bobs his head in an imbecilic fashion. Rico, Otero, Bat, and Killer Pepi move toward the office. Kid Bean stays behind, guarding the lookout and doorman, who back up against the wall. The Kid leans against the steel door from where he can cover the gambling room.

170. CLOSE SHOT DOOR TO ARNIE'S OFFICE

At the office door Rico briefly outlines his plan of campaign.

RICO:

Bat, you stay here and don't let nobody in. Pepi, if the door's locked do your stuff. Otero and I will cover you.

Pepi twists the handle of the door; it is locked. Placing his huge shoulder against it, he throws all of his tremendous bulk into a savage heave. The door springs open and Pepi falls into the room. With drawn gun Otero leaps after him. Rico follows.

171. ARNIE'S OFFICE CLOSE SHOT
Inside the office three startled men rise halfway out of their chairs: Little Arnie and his hired killers from Detroit.

172. INT. LITTLE ARNIE'S GAMBLING HOUSE CLOSE SHOT IN ARNIE'S OFFICE
Rico and his men are seen surrounding Arnie and his gangsters. Arnie is standing; now Killer Pepi's gun is against his back. Indescribable fright on his face. The two gangsters are half-collapsed in their chairs, watching the muzzles of the guns that guard them. Rico steps close to Arnie, his hat solicitously removed.

RICO (suavely):
Hello, Arnie! How's business?

The enemy are covered from either side of the room by Otero and Pepi. Rico pulls chair up to the desk and sits down, calmly taking the center of the stage.

173. INT. LITTLE ARNIE'S GAMBLING HOUSE CLOSE-UP ARNIE
Little Arnie sinks into a chair and sits with his mouth slightly open. As a rule he is imperturbable, but this cyclonic entry is too much for him. His mask slips, revealing a pale, terrified countenance.[39] He blusters:

ARNIE:
What's the game?

174. INT. LITTLE ARNIE'S GAMBLING HOUSE CLOSE SHOT
including Rico and the Arnie group. Arnie turns to his gorillas.

ARNIE:
I don't know what's wrong, but it's a private row. You guys beat it!

The Detroit gangsters, only too willing, start to get out of their chairs. They settle back when Rico speaks:

RICO:

Sit still! You guys are invited to this private party.

Although he does not move, one of them speaks:

DETROIT GANGSTER (sneering):

Suppose we don't want to stay, see?

175. INT. LITTLE ARNIE'S GAMBLING HOUSE MED. SHOT

With his maddening smile, Rico looks from Otero to Pepi, then back to the enemy.

RICO (pleasantly):

I wouldn't stop you for the world, but those boys of mine have itching fingers.

There is a long pause in which the Detroit mugs and Arnie shift uncomfortably in their chairs. Rico breaks the silence.

RICO:

Arnie, you oughta had better sense than to hire a couple of outside yaps! Especially bad shots.

176. INT. LITTLE ARNIE'S GAMBLING HOUSE CLOSE-UP RICO

Rico thrusts out his square jaw.

RICO:

You hired these mugs. They missed. Now you're through. If you ain't out of town by tomorrow mornin', you won't never leave it except in a pine box!

Arnie, completely unnerved, actually trembling, doesn't reply.

RICO (trembling):

I'm takin' over this territory . . . from now on, it's mine.

177. INT. LITTLE ARNIE'S GAMBLING HOUSE MED. CLOSE SHOT

ARNIE (bitterly):

You're growin', Rico. This is what you been after all the time, eh? I saw it in your eyes the first time I met you . . . (With unaccustomed bravado.) You're a rat, Rico. But if you think you can muscle in on me like you did on Sam Vettori, you're off your nut. I guess you forgot all about Pete Montana?

This, for an instant, stops Rico. His face assumes a worried expression as his mind weighs the possible consequences of running up against Pete Montana. Next his face hardens.

RICO:

And how's Diamond Pete gonna stop me? He may be your boss, but he ain't mine.

ARNIE (sneering):

Sam was too soft. Diamond Peter could scare him. But I ain't no Sam! Sam is through . . . now you're through, too!

178. INT. LITTLE ARNIE'S GAMBLING HOUSE CLOSE-UP RICO
Rico stands staring impersonally at Arnie and we cut to an insert to see that he is studying Arnie's fancy stickpin.

INSERT FLASH OF ARNIE'S STICKPIN

179. INT. LITTLE ARNIE'S GAMBLING HOUSE CLOSE-UP STICKPIN
in detail, as we later use the same one or its duplicate. Having impressed the design on his mind, Rico's glance lifts to Arnie's face.

RICO:

Nice stickpin you got, Arnie! I'll have to make a note of it . . . (Shows him his hand.) See my ring? Nothin' phony about my jewelry . . .

INSERT DIAMOND RING ON RICO'S FINGER
This is an exact facsimile of the ring worn by Pete Montana in scene 24.

Arnie, without glancing at the ring, just stares at Rico. Now Rico laughs:

RICO:

Better quit the racket, Arnie. You got so you can dish it out, but you can't take it no more.[40]

180. INT. LITTLE ARNIE'S GAMBLING HOUSE TRUCK SHOT
Rico motions to his men, turns, and walks out. Otero follows. Pepi backs out, covering the boss. Arnie does not move. The two Detroit gunmen sit slouched in their chairs, looking at the desk. THE CAMERA TRUCKS BACK through the door ahead of Rico. Killer Pepi starts to chuckle. It rumbles into a roar of laughter.

FADE OUT

TWELFTH SEQUENCE

FADE IN

181. INSERT SOCIETY COLUMN NOTICE

Mr. Arnold Lorch, of the North Side, has just left for Detroit where he intends to spend the summer. He was accompanied by two of his Detroit friends, who have been in Chicago for a short stay.

DISSOLVE TO:

182. PALERMO OFFICE MED. CLOSE SHOT
The society item is Scabby's work. He is hailed as a hero by Pepi, Sam Vettori, Bat, and Kid Bean. They are grouped around Scabby, who has a paper in his hand.[41] The others roar with laughter and slap Scabby on the back.

DISSOLVE TO:

183. MA MAGDALENA'S OFFICE MED. CLOSE SHOT
Repulsive old Ma Magdalena chuckles over the joke at the desk in her office.

DISSOLVE TO:

184. PEACOCK DRESSING ROOM CLOSE SHOT
DeVoss shows the paper to Joe. Both laugh. DeVoss is tickled to pieces to think that he is rid of Little Arnie. But Joe makes a vital comment which turns DeVoss into a thoughtful mood—he is probably dropped from the frying pan into the fire.

JOE:

That means you have a new partner—Little Caesar.

DISSOLVE TO:

185. EXT. CORNER OF BUILDING CLOSE-UP
Flaherty reads the notice and smiles grimly, then his eyes narrow.

DISSOLVE TO:

186. RICO'S ROOM IN LITTLE ITALY FULL SHOT
This is a dingy room in Little Italy. Rico has not yet thought of moving into more pretentious quarters.

Rico is lying on his bed, in a loud bathrobe—he is not sleeping, merely resting. Otero is seated in a chair, smoking.

187. RICO'S ROOM IN LITTLE ITALY CLOSE SHOT
Otero looks at newspaper in his hand, then speaks admiringly:

OTERO:

Now you're famous, Rico. Everybody laugh at Scabby's story.

188. RICO'S ROOM IN LITTLE ITALY CLOSE-UP RICO
Rico grins as he lies on his bed, then says:

RICO:

Yeah, Little Arnie took an awful walloping, all right. You see, Otero, 'tain't no use bein' scared of any of these big guys. The bigger they come, the harder they fall. Yeah, I ain't doin' so bad in this business so far . . . (He absentmindedly fingers his scarfpin.)

189. INSERT CLOSE-UP OF SCARFPIN EXACTLY LIKE THE ONE ARNIE WORE THE NIGHT PREVIOUS

Rico smiles, apparently thinking of his victory.[42] Now, over the SHOT, comes a knock on the door.

190. RICO'S ROOM IN LITTLE ITALY MED. CLOSE SHOT

Otero leaps across the room, standing at one side of the door, out of range of anyone shooting through the panel. He looks anxiously back to Rico, who should not be disturbed. Rico props himself on his good elbow, gazing at the door. Seeing that the boss is awake, Otero speaks:

OTERO:

Who's there?

Ritz Colonna's tough voice answers—we are not familiar enough with the voice to recognize it.

RITZ:

A couple of right guys to see Rico.

RICO:

Duck, you 'right guys, because I'm going to count three . . .

ANOTHER VOICE (Montana):

Hold your horses. This is Pete Montana.

Rico recognizes Montana's voice and motions for Otero to unbolt the door. Otero obeys, standing half behind it with his gun ready. Montana and his bodyguard enter.

Otero drags up the only two chairs in the room, placing one at the bedside, the other a little distance away. Montana sits down beside the bed. His bodyguard takes the other chair. Otero squats on the floor, back against the wall behind them.

191. RICO'S ROOM IN LITTLE ITALY   CLOSE SHOT
The brazen assurance and air of authority that so far have characterized Montana seem somewhat lacking. His manner is a bit hollow. He and Rico eye each other steadily. Montana breaks the short silence.

MONTANA:

I been watching you, Rico. Any guy that can muscle in on Sam Vettori and Little Arnie is on the up and up with me. The Big Boy thinks the same way. He sent me to talk things over with you!

Rico's mind works at lightning speed. What is this preliminary to? His glance flicks from Montana to Colonna (latter out of scene). It is unusual, to say the least, for a big shot to make any advances. Then he begins to sense the truth. Montana is getting soft. With this knowledge his arrogance grows.

RICO (affably):

Thanks. I ain't lookin' for no trouble with you, Pete.

MONTANA:

I guess we got the wrong steer, then. Some wise guys told us you was going to edge into my territory.

Rico yawns before answering calmly.

RICO:

Them guys don't know what they're talking about.

192. RICO'S ROOM IN LITTLE ITALY CLOSE-UP MONTANA
Montana's eyes open, then narrow wickedly. He is going to test Rico.

MONTANA:
You know I used to work Little Arnie's territory and by rights it's mine.

193. RICO'S ROOM IN LITTLE ITALY CLOSE SHOT
Rico's reaction is swift. He sits up and swings his feet over the edge of the bed, bringing his face close to Montana. Rico evidently has put the fear of death into all the gang leaders, for Pete draws away slightly and adds hastily:

MONTANA:
But I don't muscle in on no right guy, see? It's yours now, Rico.

RICO:
It's mine and I won't stand for no cutting in.

Montana laughs and answers with the air of a king bestowing largess, trying to keep up his position:

MONTANA:
There won't be no cuttin' in— Maybe we can team up on a couple o' jobs.

This is a tremendous concession for a man of Pete's standing and Rico is amazed. He glances toward Otero.

194. RICO'S ROOM IN LITTLE ITALY CLOSE-UP OTERO
The little Mexican's eyes are popping. He grins widely. His idol has outfaced the great Montana. (We use Otero's reaction here, as Rico would not display his triumphant feeling to Montana.)

195. RICO'S ROOM IN LITTLE ITALY MED. CLOSE-UP RICO AND MONTANA
Rico rises. Montana follows suit.

RICO:

You and me can do business.

Montana offers hand. They pump arms briefly. Rico looks down at the other's manicured fist.

INSERT CLOSE-UP OF RING ON MONTANA'S LITTLE FINGER
It is a flashy diamond and emerald creation.

Rico now glances at his own, similar ring in satisfaction, then looks up at Montana. The latter withdraws his hand.

MONTANA:

I guess we'll go. If you need any advice, come to me.

RICO:

Much obliged. A new guy has a lot to learn.

The ironic tone of his voice causes Pete to look sharply at the little man, but Rico's face is blandly innocent.

196. RICO'S ROOM IN LITTLE ITALY MED. SHOT
Otero unbolts the door. Pete leaves. His bodyguard exits after him. Otero shoots the bolt and turns to Rico, who is staring into space, visioning much greater worlds to conquer. The Mexican sums up the situation with two [*sic*] words:

OTERO:

He's scared of you.

197. CLOSE-UP RICO

RICO (laughs aloud):

Otero, you said a mouthful. He's soft. He's got so he can dish it out, but can't take it no more! It's my turn now! There's no stopping me!

FADE OUT

THIRTEENTH SEQUENCE

TIME LAPSE TITLE

FADE IN

198. INT. RICO'S ROOM LITTLE ITALY

OTERO (helping Rico to dress):
Look, Boss, you're getting up in the world. Ain't none of us ever been asked to eat with the Big Boy at his dump. Nobody ever crashed the gates but Pete Montana—see what I mean? You don't want the Big Boy to think you ain't got no class.

RICO (feeling uncomfortable; the suit is too big for him):
Yeah—they rig you up better than this in the stir. You're crazy if you think I'm going out looking like this.

OTERO (convincingly):
You look fine, Boss.

RICO:
Yeah—all I need is a napkin over my arm.

Otero tips mirror for Rico to get full length view of himself. Rico is won over.

RICO:
I guess it don't look so bad.

DISSOLVE TO:

199. INT. LIVING ROOM BIG BOY'S APARTMENT
Rico hands hat and gloves to butler.[43] He hesitates about shaking hands with Big Boy. Big Boy crosses to meet him. The host looks at Rico's swell outfit and his eyes twinkle.

BIG BOY:
Rather lit up tonight, aren't you, Rico?

RICO (self-consciously):
Yeah—I thought I'd better put on my monkey suit.

BIG BOY:

That's right, Rico, May as well learn now.

The host laughs and motions Rico to a seat. Rico takes long look around the room before sitting down.

RICO:

Some dump you've got.[44]

BIG BOY:

Yeah—I sure paid for it. See that picture over there? That set me back fifteen thousand dollars.

RICO (aghast; whistles):

Them solid gold frames sure cost dough!

The butler wheels in tea wagon with drinks. Rico takes it big.

BIG BOY (patronizingly):

Will you have a cocktail or a dash of brandy?

RICO (shaking his head):

Not me. Never touch the stuff. Never!

The butler passes humidor full of cigars. Rico takes one, lights it, and tips back his chair.

BIG BOY:

I'm gonna talk and you're not going to hear a word I say. See? This is inside dope and if it gets out it'll be just too bad for somebody.

RICO:

You know me.

BIG BOY:

All right, get this. If I didn't think a lot of you I wouldn't be asking you to come to eat with me. You're on the square, Rico, and you're a comer. You got the nerve and you're a good, steady, sober fellow . . . Pete Montana is through . . .

RICO (almost leaping out of his chair):
Yeah? And I thought he was such a big guy!

BIG BOY:
He has seen his day. If he puts up an argument it'll be just too bad.

RICO:
I'll say so.

BIG BOY:
If I said that you're a Pete Montana from now on—that you were to take over his territory and handle it in addition to your own—would you shake on it?

RICO (beside himself):
Would I? *Would* I!

BIG BOY:
All right. It's set! I'm doing a lot for you, but when I get you planted I want plenty of service.

RICO:
You'll sure get it.

BIG BOY (lifting his glass):
Permit me, then, to drink to the new boss of the North Side.

FADE OUT

FOURTEENTH SEQUENCE

TIME LAPSE TITLE[45]

FADE IN

200. RICO'S NEW APARTMENT

Rico walking up and down the room like a proud peacock and addressing Otero.

RICO:
I knew it was coming. I knew he had his eyes on me. Let me tell you—it's not only Pete Montana that's through—but the Big Boy himself.

201. INT. LIVING ROOM RICO'S NEW APARTMENT
CLOSE-UP RICO
as he continues:

RICO:
The Big Boy himself—he ain't what he used to be, neither. Pretty soon *he* won't be able to take it and then . . . *watch me!*[46]

202. INT. LIVING ROOM RICO'S NEW APARTMENT MED. SHOT
The butler comes in, announcing.

BUTLER:
Mr. Massara to see you, sir.

RICO:
Send him in.

Butler exits. Rico hastens to a chair at the fireplace, sits down, quickly takes out another panatela, unwraps it, and inserts it in his mouth. All this is done very obviously to impress Joe.

Now Joe enters, stops in the doorway, takes in the apartment, letting his gaze rest on each object individually. Rico is watching him from out of the corners of his eyes.

JOE:
Gee whiz, Rico . . . what a palace!

Rico, who has pretended not to notice the other's entrance, now looks up.

RICO (with an air of boredom):
Oh, hello, Joe! Yeah, it's a good joint. What you expect—ain't I got twenty grand tied up in it?

JOE (coming nearer):
Hello, Otero! How do you feel, baby?

OTERO:
First rate.

RICO:
Sit down, Joe.

JOE (as he goes to fireplace and takes chair):
You sure I'm good enough to sit in such a swell chair? (Sits down.)

RICO:
Cut the comedy, Joe. (Turning to Otero.) Screw, Otero. I gotta talk to Joe private.

OTERO (with an obliging smile):
Sure. (Crosses to door. While he is doing this, Rico offers the box of cigars to Joe.)

RICO:
Cigar, Joe?

JOE:
Thanks!

By this time Otero has gained the door, exits.

203. INT. LIVING ROOM RICO'S NEW APARTMENT MED. CLOSE SHOT RICO AND JOE

RICO (closely studying Joe):
Well, surprise you to hear from me? I sorta thought it would be nice to have a little talk . . . like old times.

JOE (ill at ease; he tries an air of innocence):
It certainly is nice to see you . . . especially like this!

RICO (surveying Joe):
You're lookin' good, too, Joe. Only a little too fat, maybe. Livin' easy, kinda?

JOE (smiling):
Not *that* easy . . . Dancin' is no cinch.

RICO (with a queer half-smile):
But you ain't complainin'?

JOE (fearing what is to come; his smile dies away):
No, I ain't complainin'.

RICO:
That's good. (Sits back in his chair.) You're right about dancin'. Nothin' like relaxation. Yeah, dancin' is fine for a—sideline.[47] (Looks at Joe from under drawn eyebrows, studying the effect of his words upon him.)

JOE:
What's the difference, Rico? As long as I ain't kickin', why should you kick?

RICO (stroking his chin):
Who's kickin'? Only, should a young guy like you be wastin' his time? I kinda took a pride in you, Joe . . . brought you into the gang . . . pushed you ahead . . . But now you're gettin' to be a sissy.

204. INT. LIVING ROOM RICO'S NEW APARTMENT
MED. CLOSE-UP JOE

JOE (uneasily shifting in his chair):
We gonna start that again? Can't you just forget about me?

205. INT. LIVING ROOM RICO'S NEW APARTMENT
CLOSE-UP INCLUDING BOTH

RICO (with a certain softness in his voice):
How can I forget about my pal, Joe? We started off together—we gotta keep on goin' along together. Who else have I got to give a hang about? (Now he jumps up, goes over to Joe.) I need *you*, Joe. Just before you came, I was over to see the Big Boy. He handed me the whole *North Side*. But it's too big for one man to handle alone . . . I need somebody—a guy like you—somebody I can trust, somebody to work in with me.

Joe shakes his head.

JOE:

It can't be me, Buddy. I've quit.

Fierce rage takes possession of Rico's face. He grabs Joe by the shoulder:

RICO:

You didn't quit! Nobody ever quit me. Get that! You're still in my gang. I don't care how many fancy dames you got stickin' on to you. That skirt can go hang. It's *her* that's made a softy outa you.

JOE (a menacing look coming into his face):

You lay off Olga, Rico!

RICO (furiously):

I ain't layin' off her. I'm after her. She an' me can't both have you. One of us has gotta lose—an' it ain't gonna be me! There's ways of stoppin' that dame . . . !

As he says the last sentence, he makes his old significant gesture of reaching for his gun.

JOE (terror-stricken as he interprets the movement):

You're crazy! Leave her out of this . . .

RICO (his face distorted with rage now; he is fairly shrieking):

It's curtains for her, see? She's through . . . she's out of the way . . . that's what she is!

JOE (drawing back; almost insanely):

You're lyin'. You wouldn't . . .

RICO:

I *wouldn't?* I'll show you . . . that dirty, painted-up . . .

JOE (almost shrieking):
I love her! We're in love! Don't that mean nothin' to you?

RICO:
Nothin'! Less than nothin'! Love—soft stuff! When she's got you, you ain't safe . . . you know too much. I ain't takin' no chances. You're stayin' here!

JOE:
I'm not![48]

RICO (gripping his shoulder):
You move an' it's suicide . . . suicide for *both* o' you!

206. INT. LIVING ROOM RICO'S NEW APARTMENT CLOSE-UP JOE

Joe, almost paralyzed with fear, sinks back against the chair, drops into it. He shuts his eyes and puts a guarding hand up against his face.

JOE (hoarsely):
No . . . no, no . . .

207. INT. LIVING ROOM RICO'S NEW APARTMENT MED CLOSE SHOT

Rico, a look of evil satisfaction on his face, stands over the boy, closely studying him. He is about to say something, as the telephone rings from outside the room. Irritated, Rico glaces toward the door. Then he starts off, with a suspicious glance at Joe. Joe rises—instantly Rico turns and roughly thrusts him back in his chair.

RICO:
Don't you move or I'll . . .

Joe, limp, remains in his chair. We see Rico exiting through door leading to bedroom.

208. INT. LIVING ROOM RICO'S NEW APARTMENT CLOSE-UP JOE

as he sits, trembling in his chair, his face moving convulsively.

JOE:

No . . . no . . .

Over the SHOT, from the other room we hear Rico's voice at the telephone. His words are unintelligible.[49] Joe, once more, now hysterically:

JOE:

No . . . Olga . . . no . . .

Suddenly he jumps up, looks around—indescribable fear on his face—once more looks at the door from behind which we hear Rico's voice, and blindly dashes toward door.

209. INT. LIVING ROOM RICO'S NEW APARTMENT FULL SHOT

Joe dashes to door, through which he had originally come—his movements unsteady—and bursts through it. Hold SHOT after his exit. Rico's words still continue on the telephone.

FADE OUT

FOURTEENTH SEQUENCE[50]

FADE IN

210. INT. OLGA'S APARTMENT LATE AFTERNOON LIVING ROOM MED. SHOT

This is a modest enough, very orderly little living room in Olga's apartment. As we fade in, Olga is nervously walking up and down the room. From the impatient little noises she makes with her tongue, from her manner of repeatedly glancing at her wristwatch, from her occasional slapping of her palm against the knuckle of her other hand, we are instantly aware of her impatience and agitation. Now, apparently unable to control herself any longer, she rushes to the telephone.

211. INT. OLGA'S APARTMENT LIVING ROOM CLOSE-UP OLGA

OLGA (calling into telephone):
Greenhill 0139.

There is a moment's wait, during which she bites her lips, her face again and again assuming a tense, listening expression. Finally there is a voice at the other end.

OLGA (her voice trembling with excitement):
Bronze Peacock? This is Olga Stassoff . . . yes, Olga . . . Mr. DeVoss? Listen, has Joe been around there? (Her face drops; the answer is apparently disappointing.) Oh . . . ! I just thought . . . He's been gone all afternoon . . . Went to see Rico . . .

It is plain that DeVoss is trying to calm her fears, because Olga now answers.

OLGA:
It's just that I'm worried . . . I don't know why . . . but he was to be here an hour ago and hasn't come yet . . . I'm afraid . . .

DeVoss again says something. Now Olga essays a little laugh. Passing her hand over her forehead, she says:

OLGA:
Yes, I suppose it's all right . . . It was just a funny feeling I had . . . Thanks, Mr. DeVoss. Good-bye! (Limply puts down receiver.)

Now, from outside a bell is heard. Its sound is a distinct shock to Olga, who jumps up in instant terror. She holds her hands to her breast, gasping for breath.[51]

212. INT. OLGA'S APARTMENT LIVING ROOM MED. SHOT
Olga hurries across the room to the door. This door opens directly on the staircase landing, without a hallway—a not uncommon feature of old-fashioned apartment houses. She tears the door open.

213. INT. OLGA'S APARTMENT LIVING ROOM MED. CLOSE SHOT

as Olga is opening the door. Joe bursts in, out of breath, his face pale as a sheet. He tries to speak, but words fail to come from him. He stands in the doorway for a second, his hand on the outside knob, then thrusts himself into the room, closing the door behind him. He leans against it with his two palms against it. He stares at Olga with eyes wide open, clouded by terror.

OLGA:

Joe . . . Joey . . . What is it? What's the matter?

Joe gasps for breath. Then his hand shoots out, the words wheezing out of him:

JOE:

We gotta go . . . Come on . . . Hurry!

OLGA:

But Joe, you're . . .

JOE (frantic with fear):

What are you standing there for? Didn't you hear me? Hurry! Hurry!

OLGA:

Yes, Joey . . . Just let me get my things . . . (Goes up to him, putting her hand on his arm in sudden alarm.) Honey . . . you're going to faint in a minute.

JOE (thrusts her arm away; almost hysterically; shaking his head):

No, I'll be all right . . . Let's get out of here . . . We . . . Rico . . .

His voicing of the name seems to bring back memories of his visit. His face distorts; his eyelids droop. He sinks against the table standing next to the wall.

OLGA (herself blanching at the name):
What'd he do to you? Oh, I knew it! Didn't I know it?

JOE (desperately struggling to overcome his dizziness; his voice rising and falling away; feverishly):
He, Rico . . . told me you and I gotta quit . . . That he'll kill you 'less I stick with him . . . I ran away . . . Don't you see we gotta go . . . ? Anywhere! Anyplace . . . out o' town . . . so long as we get away . . .

During his speech, Olga stands before him, slowly shaking her head. Now Joe stares at her.

JOE:
No? You're . . . not . . . coming?

OLGA:
No! That's not the way!

JOE (grasping her arm):
Olga, we've got to . . . You don't know that guy . . . You're . . . Olga . . . Please . . .

OLGA:
No! Sit down, Joey . . . We've got to think . . .

JOE (shrieking):
I don't want to think. I don't want to sit down. You're . . . you're comin' . . . (He makes as though to grab her arm.)

OLGA (catching his hand and pinning it down against his body; there is a great firmness and determination in her voice):
Don't you see that would be no use? Where could we go? Where could we run to? There's no place he wouldn't find us. (Staring at Joe fixedly.) Only one thing for us to do. *Flaherty!*

JOE (his jaw drops; he stares at the girl; then):

You crazy? Do you think that'd save us? *Flaherty!* That's worse than suicide. I can't do it, I won't do it . . . not if both of us have to die a million times . . .

OLGA (firmly):

I can do it! The gang must go. Rico must go. I want my happiness. I want you. We'll never have any peace till Rico is gone . . . I'm *going* to do it!

214. INT. LIVING ROOM

Olga starts toward bedroom where telephone is. Joe guesses her intention and tries to stop her.

JOE:

Olga . . . stay here . . . don't . . .

But she is quicker than he is and gets into bedroom and slams door shut before he can stop her.

215. CLOSE-UP BEDROOM SIDE OF DOOR

Olga is locking door. On other side of door, we hear Joe pounding.

JOE (yelling):

Olga . . . open the door . . . don't call Flaherty . . . Olga! Please . . . Rico'll kill us both.

216. INT. BEDROOM CLOSE SHOT OLGA AT PHONE

OLGA:

Park 1000 . . .

Outside the door, Joe is pounding and yelling.

OLGA:

Headquarters? I want Sergeant Flaherty!

217. CLOSE SHOT JOE LIVING ROOM
As he hears the name, Joe renews his efforts to batter down door.

218. CLOSE SHOT OLGA BEDROOM

OLGA:
Sergeant Flaherty? This is Olga Stassoff . . . I've got Joe Massara with me . . . in my apartment, 17 Edgelow Drive . . . He wants to talk to you . . . Hurry . . .

Now she lets the telephone drop and sinks back exhausted.

CUT TO:

219. INT. DETECTIVE HEADQUARTERS CLOSE-UP FLAHERTY
He is just replacing the receiver on its hook; he stares into the mouthpiece for a moment, lost in thought. Then a smile comes to his face and he turns to his partner:

FLAHERTY:
Come on, sweetheart!

220. INT. DETECTIVE HEADQUARTERS MED. CLOSE SHOT
The other detective, his partner, rises. Yawns.

SECOND DETECTIVE:
Who's giving the cocktail party?

FLAHERTY (with immense satisfaction in his voice):
Joe Massara.

The other detective's eyes open wide in surprise. He whistles softly.

FLAHERTY:
Got the artillery on you?[52] (He examines his own holster.)

CUT TO:

221. INT. OLGA'S APARTMENT LIVING ROOM MED. CLOSE SHOT

JOE:

You shouldn't have done it . . . you shouldn't have . . .

OLGA (who is standing near the table):

There was no other way . . . no other right way . . .

JOE:

It's the rope for me.

OLGA (Firmly):

No! Not if you turn state's evidence. We'll make them promise that . . .

CUT TO:

222. EXT. OLGA'S APARTMENT HOUSE VERY LONG SHOT

Olga's house is one of many in a row of brownstone fronts. A machine draws up. As it slows down and before it has a chance to stop two men jump out of it and dash up the stoop. Only now does the machine come to a halt.

NOTE: The two men running up the steps are Rico and Otero. But as it is essential for the audience to believe they are Flaherty and his partner, the shot should be taken in such a manner as to make the two figures unrecognizable.[53]

223. INT. HALLWAY OLGA'S APARTMENT HOUSE

Olga's house is a walk-up affair. It is a dark, winding staircase, full of obscuring shadows. We see the two men rushing up the steps. Again we must not be able to tell who they are.

224. INT. OLGA'S LIVING ROOM MEDIUM SHOT

Joe sits up in his chair. He is hearing the footsteps outside.

JOE (teeth chattering with fright):

It's them . . .

He jumps up and cowers against the wall.

OLGA (also listening):

Yes. (Starts for door, giving Joe's hand a passing touch.) Stick it out! You can do it!

JOE (catching hold of her hand):

Wait . . . Olga, I . . .

But it is too late. At this moment the door bursts open, under the battering strength of Otero's shoulder. Instantly he steps through the crack . . . followed by Rico.

OTERO:

There he is . . . the yellow double-crosser . . . Give it to 'im, Rico!

225. INT. OLGA'S LIVING ROOM CLOSE SHOT

Olga reels back, then frantically throws her arms around Joe. She is about to scream, but her terror is so great that the sound freezes on her lips.

226. INT. OLGA'S LIVING ROOM CLOSE-UP RICO

Rico reaches into his pocket, then slowly raises his hand. The muzzle of the gun sticking through the cloth of the pocket is pointed at Joe. Rico's face is twisted into an awful mask of pain.

227. INT. OLGA'S LIVING ROOM CLOSE-UP JOE

He stands against the wall, arms spread out. In the failing light of the afternoon he resembles a figure crucified. He shuts his eyes, waiting for the shot.

228. INT. OLGA'S LIVING ROOM MED. SHOT

Olga is about to rush at Rico, who still stands there with his gun poised, watching Joe. Otero, similarly aiming his pocketed gun at her, holds her in check. Joe now staggers, stumbles; he is on his knees, eyes closed, his arms again shoot out in front of him in a piteous gesture.[54]

JOE (screaming):
Shoot! Shoot! Get it over with!

Rico draws back—his hand drops—he can not pull the trigger.

RICO (in a gruff voice, to Otero):
Let's go, Otero . . . *I can't!*

OTERO (shooting Rico a look full of surprise that instantly changes to hatred):
You're gettin' soft, too!

He wheels around, jerks out his gun, and fires at Joe. Rico hits the little man's arm up just in time and the bullet goes wild. Joe staggers back, holding his wounded shoulder.

CUT TO:

229. EXT. APARTMENT HOUSE MED. SHOT
Another machine stops. Flaherty and his partner, accompanied by a third dick, jump out of it. At this moment a shot rings out above, followed by Olga's scream. The three detectives halt for an instant, look up toward the window from where the sounds issued, then dash up the steps, disappearing through the door of the house.

CUT BACK TO:

230. INT. APARTMENT HOUSE MED. SHOT
Rico is just wresting the automatic away from Otero, his look menacing the Mexican.

RICO:
Gimme that, you . . .

The Mexican seems to be putting up a fight. The two men struggle for the possession of the gun. Rico succeeds in tearing the weapon from the Mexican and they dash to door. But at this moment, from outside, we hear voices.

FLAHERTY'S PARTNER'S VOICE:

What floor?

Rico stops short, stares at the door, like an animal at bay. Now, from outside, another voice answers the first:

FLAHERTY'S VOICE:

The third! Come on, boys!

Rico leaps back, wheels around, dashes to window, Otero after him.[55]

231. INT. OLGA'S LIVING ROOM CLOSE SHOT AT WINDOW
Hastily throwing up the window, Rico crawls through, followed by Otero. Outside the window can be seen a fire escape.

232. EXT. FIRE ESCAPE OLGA'S APARTMENT
With unbelievable agility, Rico is dashing down the iron steps of the fire escape, Otero in his wake.

233. INT. OLGA'S ROOM MED. SHOT
Flaherty and the two detectives have just dashed into the room. Flaherty stops short, rushes up to Joe, who is cowering, still holding his shoulder.

FLAHERTY:

They get you, Joe? Who was it?

Joe looks up at the cop, defiance in his eyes. Then he suddenly looks away.

OLGA (shrieking):

Otero . . . It was Otero . . . He and Rico! (Dramatically pointing to window.) There!

234. INT. OLGA'S LIVING ROOM CLOSE-UP FLAHERTY
With snap of his fingers, Flaherty commands the other two detectives:

FLAHERTY:
Get 'em, boys!

235. INT. OLGA'S LIVING ROOM MED SHOT
The two detectives yank out their guns, rush to the window, and, crawling through, disappear. Flaherty turns to Joe:

FLAHERTY:
Well, Joe—ready to talk now?

Joe answers nothing, keeping his eyes on the floor.

236. INT. OLGA'S LIVING ROOM CLOSE SHOT
Olga rushes up to Flaherty.

OLGA (beating her breast with her fist to give emphasis to her excited exclamation):
I'll talk! It was Rico's gang that held up the Bronze Peacock . . . It was Rico that shot McClure . . . the dirty, low sneaking . . . (Her voice rising.) Joe will tell you! Ask him! He knows it was Rico . . .

FLAHERTY (stepping close to Joe):
Let's have it, Joe. Was it Rico?

Joe is silent. Flaherty's eyes challenge him. Unable to tear his eyes away from the almost hypnotic gaze of the detective, Joe finally drops his eyes. Almost perceptibly he nods his head. Then he nods once more. A look of triumph comes over Flaherty's face; now he nods, then dashes to telephone.

237. INT. OLGA'S LIVING ROOM CLOSE-UP FLAHERTY AT PHONE

FLAHERTY:

Park 1000 . . . (He waits for a second, then speaks rapidly into the mouthpiece.) Hello—Jack? Round up the Palermo gang. I got enough on 'em to use a mile of rope. Anyway—*get Rico!*

DISSOLVE INTO:

238. EXT. POLICE STATION LONG SHOT

Two emergency police cars, loaded to the running boards with reserves, tear out of the station, sirens screaming. The cops are armed with riot guns.

DISSOLVE:

239. EXT. SIGNAL BOX MED. CLOSE SHOT

The cop is listening to a message over the phone and blowing his whistle loudly at the same time. The first man hangs up, snaps the box shut, and runs out, motioning for the second to follow.

DISSOLVE:

240. EXT. ALLEY MED. CLOSE SHOT

Rico and Otero shoot into the picture and run toward the corner of the alley and street. They halt IN CAMERA. In the distance a police siren is heard.

RICO (cautious; looking around suspiciously):

Now we got to watch our step. The cops are sure to be cruising around this street.[56]

They step to the corner—nervous, dangerous. Rico halts for an instant:

RICO:

This is what I get for liking a guy too much . . . !

241. EXT. ALLEY LONG SHOT

Rico and Otero dash straight across the street, looking

neither to left nor right, aiming for the alley on the other side. Halfway to their destination a cop appears out of a doorway three or four houses away and starts running toward them, blowing his whistle and tugging at his gun.

COP:

Halt!

The two gangsters instantly take to their heels and beat it for the shelter of the alley. Otero takes a flying shot at the cop, who keeps on.

A few yards down the alley Otero stops, waits for the cop to appear, and shoots when he barges around the corner of the building. The cop staggers forward three or four steps and drops to his knees. He has been hit in the leg.

242. EXT. ALLEY LONG SHOT

past the cop who calmly steadies his gun with both hands and fires from the kneeling position at the fleeing men in background.

243. EXT. ALLEY TRUCK SHOT

holding Otero and Rico. Otero twists sideways, looks at Rico in surprise, stops, and drops his gun. He keeps on walking, holding his stomach. Forgetting everything else, even the bullets which continue to sing close to them, Rico puts his arm around the little man and holds him up. After a few steps, Otero pulls away.

OTERO (with doglike devotion):

Run, Rico, run. They got me. I can't feel nothin'.

Rico swings him over his shoulder and starts to run heavily, keeping a telephone pole between him and the disabled cop who is still shooting. The sound of police sirens comes from every direction. Rico dodges around the angle of a board fence. Otero hits him feebly in the face, crying:

OTERO:

Let me down. Get away yourself. I'm done for!

Reluctantly Rico places Otero on his feet. The little man gives the boss an eloquent look, spins around, and falls flat on his back. TRUCK BACK TO A WIDER SHOT. Rico leaps a board fence. A bunch of cops charge around the corner and spread out as skirmishers when they see Otero's body.[57]

DISSOLVE INTO:

244. SIGN

CLUB
P
A
L
E
R
M
O
DANCING

It is toward evening and the sign is flashing on and off. Through the sign,

DISSOLVE INTO:

245. INT. CLUB PALERMO SAM'S OFFICE MED. CLOSE SHOT

Sam is sitting playing solitaire. In the background can be seen Killer Pepi, Kid Bean, and a few lesser members of the gang. These other boys are seated at a table, shooting crap. Ad lib remarks, accompanying the game:

THE GANG:

Hey, keep your hands off that dough! That's mine!
Aw, rest your jaw!

Now the door is torn open and Scabby rushes into the room, breathless.

SCABBY (almost screaming):

Sam . . . !

Sam, without looking up, says casually:

SAM:

'Lo, Scabby! Wanna bottle o' wine?

SCABBY:

Wine? (Rushing up to Sam, screaming.) Joe Massara . . . They nabbed him on the McClure business and he squawked . . . !

Excited exclamations from the boys. They all gather around the table. Sam's jaw falls and he runs his hands over his face in a bewildered way.

SAM (with a groan):

Oh!

SCABBY (continuing):

Rico tried to get 'im and now the bulls are after *him* . . . They got Otero . . . !

PEPI (in a hushed whisper):

Otero!

A silence falls on the group for an instant. Next Kid Bean lets out an inarticulate cry of terror, runs to the closet door, and, wrenching it open, grabs an automatic and small box of ammunition. The others follow suit. Only Sam sits quietly, his face still covered with his hands.

SCABBY (impatiently taking hold of his shoulder):

Sam! Don't you get me? It's all off! What are you sittin' there for?

SAM (shrugging his shoulders):

What else can I do? No use running. They'd get me anyway.

SCABBY:

You're outta your head! Get up! Let's beat it!

SAM:

No use . . . [58]

SCABBY:

You fool, you're gonna . . .

Now a siren is heard from outside. Scabby, no longer in a mood to argue, starts for the closet arsenal.

SAM (calling after him):

Scabby, if you get away . . . pop Rico for me. It's his doin' . . . He muscled in on me . . . He's busted us all. Pop him, Scabby, for old Sam!

Scabby, instead of answering, rushes over to Sam and thrusts an automatic into his hand.

SCABBY:

Here . . . be a man!

One or two of the boys have by this time gained the secret panel. There is a sudden rush of feet on the stairs—now a volley of shots. Next Bat Carillo bursts into the room. He sticks his hand around the doorjamb and lets go the remainder of a clip. The shots are answered from outside.

BAT:

The bulls!

Bat dashes across the room, toward the secret panel. As he does so, he fires two or three more shots. Now Scabby jumps through the panel, after Bat, sliding it in place behind him. Sam, dazed and petrified, puts his back to the wall and faces the door. Flaherty steps cautiously into the room, sees Sam with the gun, and steps back. He calls from the hall.

FLAHERTY:

Sam—better give up—drop that gun before we start shooting!

Sam obeys—the gun making a loud clatter on the floor. Flaherty comes into the room holding his service revolver in front of him. He beckons and two big cops appear.

FLAHERTY (indicating Sam):
Put the cuffs on him!

Sam stupidly hold out his hands, saying with a final flash of cunning.

SAM:
You ain't got nothin' on me!

FLAHERTY (laughs grimly):
No? Nor on Rico, either. He's next![59]

Flaherty runs out of the room as the cops snap the bracelets on Sam's wrists.

DISSOLVE:

246. INT. MA MAGDALENA'S FRUIT STORE MED. SHOT
Ma Magdalena is talking to a patrolman in the fruit store (perhaps the man we saw at the signal box). Another cop comes out of the office. Both men have drawn guns. The second man speaks.

SECOND PATROLMAN:
I looked everyplace. Nobody here.

FIRST PATROLMAN:
Listen, Ma. If you see Rico or the other little guy you'd better let us know pronto![60]

The old hag bobs her head. The cops exit. Ma snarls after them. Rico's head appears in the office door.

RICO:
Sssssssssssss.

Ma turns, see Rico, and hobbles to him as fast as she can move.

247. MA MAGDALENA'S OFFICE CLOSE SHOT
Rico steps back into the office as the old woman comes in. She looks shrewdly at him.

MA:

So, you sneaked in the back way? Well, you got yourself in a nice fix.

RICO (grinning):

Who told you?

MA:

The police were just here searching the place.

Rico's expression changes. His face falls into lines of worry and sorrow.

RICO:

They got Otero.

Ma Magdalena only shrugs and moves across the office to open the secret door to the hideout. Rico follows, talking.

RICO:

I'm going to stay here a day or two. Then I'll want a car!

Rico goes through the narrow entrance into the cubby-hole and switches on the light.

248. INT. HIDEOUT CLOSE SHOT
shooting past Rico and Ma Magdalena, who stands in the opening holding on to the swinging shelves. Rico makes a swift survey of the tiny room and sits down on the cot.

MA:

It's gonna cost you big, because I'm takin' big chances.

RICO (in grand manner):

Well, you got ten grand I planted here. Help yourself.

Ma edges the door closed. She knows that Rico is wholly at her mercy and she means to take full advantage of it.

MA:

I'll give you a hundred and fifty dollars when you're ready to start.

Rico is instantly aroused and speaks angrily. The hag closes the door to a mere slit.

RICO:

You're crazy. I need plenty. Most of my dough is cached in my apartment and there won't be no chance of gettin' it.

MA:

One hundred and fifty's all you get. Take it or leave it.

RICO (enraged, starts toward her as if to strangle her):

Why, you dirty, double-crossin', thievin' old hag—I'll—

MA:

I'm the only one knows where it's hid. (Rico glares. She backs away from him.) Go ahead—kill me and you'll never get out of town. (Through the crack of door.) One hundred and fifty is all you get![61]

The door is slammed shut. Rico springs toward it, all his fury exhausting itself as he bangs with his fists on the closed door.

FADE OUT

FIFTEENTH SEQUENCE

FADE INTO

249. INSERT CLUB PALERMO SIGN

CLUB
P
A
L
E
R
M
O
DANCING

As we see the sign it is dead, no longer flashing on and off. Most of the electric bulbs are broken or completely gone. Several of the letters are missing. Broken bits of wires hang loose from the sign. The glass portions of it are broken, the tin casing dented. From this, SLOWLY PAN DOWN TO:

250. EXT. CLUB PALERMO MAIN DOOR CLOSE SHOT

Over the padlocked door is the painted sign Club Palermo—weather-beaten, dirty. On the door, both windows are cracked; the curtain hangs loosely, flapping in the wind. On one of the windows a sign:

TO LET
APPLY TO OWNER
MA MAGDALENA

FRUIT AND VEGETABLES
101 FRONT STREET

DISSOLVE INTO:

251. EXT. LODGING HOUSE CLOSE SHOT DOOR[62]

This is another door, totally different in character—really just a niche in the wall with a dark hallway behind it. Suspended over the door on chairs which creak rustily is the sign:

CLEAN BEDS 25!

From this,

DISSOLVE INTO:

252. INT. LODGING HOUSE GENERAL SHOT

A dark, murky, evil-looking place—two long rows of cots fill the room, with hardly enough space to walk between them. In a corner of the room, under a feeble, yellowish, single electric light, sit three nondescript men, their chairs tilted against the wall. The one in the middle is reading a newspaper. The cots are mostly filled—only a few of them are still empty. The room is silent, except for an occasional snore, a mumbled word or two, the creaking of a cot. Now CAMERA TRUCKS UP:

253. INT. LODGING HOUSE TRUCK SHOW

The CAMERA TRUCKS PAST a few of the beds, showing the occupants. Most of them are lying with their clothes on. The effect is one of squalidness, misery. The CAMERA SLOWLY MOVES UP to the three men sitting against the wall.

254. INT. LODGING HOUSE CLOSE SHOT

We see a group (the three men) sitting against the wall. One of them is smoking a battered old corncob pipe. The middle one, an old man with bleary, nearsighted eyes, is holding a newspaper close to his face. The third man is sitting with his eyes closed, chewing tobacco.

MAN WITH PIPE:

And you knew him?

MAN WITH PAPER:

I know 'im. He was always no good. He was mean, Sam Vettori was, so now he got what was comin' to him!

THIRD MAN (impatiently):
Well, what's it say in the paper?

MAN WITH PAPER (painfully reading the items):
"Former gang chief faints on scaffold. After a futile battle in court, Sam Vettori, former gang leader, today presented a pitiful figure as the hangman's noose was placed around his neck."

Now CAMERA PANS OVER to a bed a foot or two away from the group with the paper.

255. INT. LODGING HOUSE CLOSE-UP RICO
He is lying on his bed in his clothes. These clothes are ragged. There is a battered cap near him; a week's stubble covers his face. He rises, leans on his elbows, snorts with contempt, and mutters to himself: "Faints, eh . . . ? He was always yellow. He could dish it out but he could never take it . . . " He giggles with a drunken leer on his face. Then he produces a whiskey bottle. Drinks. Then, still to himself: "They could say a lotta things 'bout me in the old days, but they couldn't call me yellow . . . !" Now the voice of the old man floats over this CLOSE-UP of Rico.

VOICE OF MAN WITH PAPER:
Listen . . . "Little Caesar has never been found. He is hiding like a rat in his hole. The once swaggering braggart of the underworld wilted in the face of real danger and showed the world his cowardice, thus contradicting his oft-repeated boast that he could dish it out and take it too. When the moment arose, Rico couldn't take it! Meteoric as his rise from the gutter has been, it was inevitable that he should return there . . . "

VOICE OF MAN WITH PIPE:
Just the same, he was the real leader of that gang.

VOICE OF MAN WITH PAPER:

> Don't you believe it! Sam was rotten but *he* was the real head. Rico didn't have the nerve and he didn't have the brains . . . He was yellow, like the paper says. That's what Rico was . . .

As Rico hears these words, he springs into a sitting position on the bed; an ugly, threatening expression comes to his face. He leaps up, is about to start toward the group. Then his face clouds; he looks at the whiskey bottle still in his hand, looks at it long, and nods his head as though saying to himself: "I'm not the same man anymore! This is the cause of it!" Then his eyes run down his clothes, his entire figure. Dropping the whiskey bottle on the bed, he starts toward the group.

256. INT. LODGING HOUSE MED. CLOSE SHOT GROUP

MAN WITH PAPER:

> He was no good . . . No, sir, he couldn't take it, nohow!

Now Rico walks into the picture. For an instant there is the old firmness in his face. His voice is strong as he shoots out his hand with the imperious command:

RICO:

> Let's have that paper!

The old man looks up in surprise and is about to resent this, but Rico's look defeats him. Without a word, he hands over the paper.

257. INT. LODGING HOUSE CLOSE-UP RICO READING THE PAPER

INSERT

> Little Caesar has never been found. He is hiding like a rat in his hole. The once

swaggering braggart of the underworld wilted in the face of real danger and . . .

Rico's nervous hands crush the paper savagely, his rage dominating him. He stares at it. And as he stares, the INSERT SLOWLY DISSOLVES INTO:

INSERT

Little Caesar faces death with contempt. Bandello exhibits the cold nerve of an underworld king as he stands on the scaffold, flinging a laughing challenge into the . . .

258. INT. LODGING HOUSE CLOSE-UP RICO
The thought suddenly elates him with an almost insane longing to see himself as a hero, a superman in the face of death. His eyes gleam. A crazy smile illumines his face.

259. INT. LODGING HOUSE CLOSE SHOT GROUP
Now Rico suddenly pulls himself together, takes another look at the paper, crushes it, and flings it at the old man. Turning, he dashes out of picture. HOLD SHOT on the three men, staring after him.

DISSOLVE INTO:

260. EXT. POLICE STATION NIGHT
Rico comes to the front of the police station and pauses. He has been soft too long for his bravado to last. There is a mental struggle and his ego wins, though an element of fear remains. He heads hesitatingly into the station.

261. INT. POLICE STATION MED. SHOT
This is an outlying station on the South Side. It is nearing midnight and the desk sergeant is alone. He is writing in a big ledger.

Rico, rubbing his hands in the warm air, is walking toward the desk. He stops in front of the sergeant, who does not look up. Rico coughs. The sergeant raises his eyes. One swift glance and he speaks:

SERGEANT (gruffly):
Outside! All filled up. You can't flop here, tramp.

A reporter joins them, coming from a small room inside the building. He looks disdainfully at the tramp and leans against the desk, prepared to bait the defenseless bo.

262. CLOSE SHOT
Rico looks appealingly from the sergeant to the reporter, then back to the former. He does not know what to do in face of this unexpected reception.

RICO (faintly):
But . . .

SERGEANT (belligerently):
You gonna get out or do you want to get thrown out?

263. INT. POLICE STATION CLOSE-UP RICO
Rico cannot understand it and makes funny little hopeless gesture.

RICO (great sincerity):
Take me. I'm givin' myself up. I am Rico.

SERGEANT:
Rico? What d'ya mean—Rico?

RICO:
Little Caesar! That's who I am.

SERGEANT (laughing):
Yeah! I'm Napoleon!

264. INT. POLICE STATION CLOSE SHOT

The sergeant points his pen at the ragged apparition and speaks to the reporter:

SERGEANT (laughing):

That's one for your paper.

They both laugh. The reporter comes close to Rico, sniffs his breath, and makes an exaggerated shudder. Then he points to his own head with a twiggling motion of his finger.

REPORTER:

Plain bugs, Sergeant. Rico never took a drink in his life. Besides, he's hiding down in South America, spending the million bucks he got away with.

Half rising from his chair, the sergeant says with an air of finality:

SERGEANT:

I'll give you three to get outside!

Stunned, Rico looks from one to the other, then slowly turns and shambles toward the door.

SERGEANT (to reporter):

That's the sixth guy in the last year who's come in here full of sheep-dip and said he was Rico.

265. INT. POLICE STATION MED. CLOSE-UP RICO

Rico starts to open the door but stops, thinks a moment, then fishes in his vest pocket and pulls out the diamond ring. The sight of it seems to transform him and he makes his last dramatic gesture. With a sweep of his arm, he throws the ring at the Sergeant.

RICO:

All right! But give that to Detective Flaherty with Rico's compliments. He'll remember it!

There is something of his old voice in the words. He pulls the door open and exits.

266. INT. POLICE STATION CLOSE SHOT

The ring rolls over and over down the sergeant's slanting desk and finally falls on the floor. The sergeant gets out of his chair and grunts as he bends to pick it up. He looks casually at it and hands it to the reporter.

SERGEANT:

Want some ten-cent-store jewelry?

The reporter starts to toss it back, then becomes aware of the weight of the ring, and examines it closely with growing excitement.

REPORTER:

Ten-cent store, your grandma! This is real. This . . . Rico's ring! Where'd he go?

The reporter starts for the door on a run. The sergeant gazes after him with open mouth; beginning to feel uncomfortable, he decides to take no chances and rings the bell loudly for the reserves. Picking up the phone, he speaks quickly:

SERGEANT:

Give me Flaherty at headquarters in a hurry!

DISSOLVE TO:

267. EXT. STREET DOLLY SHOT

With shoulders hunched against the wind, Rico is walking along a street in an industrial district. Faintly, we hear the scream of a police siren.

268. EXT. ANOTHER STREET LONG SHOT

A police car comes careening around a corner on two wheels. Siren is screaming.

269. EXT. CLOSE SHOT BACK SEAT MOVING POLICE CAR
Flaherty and two other detectives are on the back seat.

DETECTIVE:
Are they daffy at that Kenwood station, or do you think it's really him?

FLAHERTY (grimly):
I don't know. But I'm not taking any chances. (A pause.) If it's Rico, I'm going to shoot first and ask questions later.

THIRD DETECTIVE:
That's how Rico always does business.[63]

270. EXT. STREET LONG SHOT RICO
Still trudging along. Police siren grows louder. He stops, looks over his shoulder in direction of sound, starts to walk again. He is passing a big illuminated billboard: The Laughing, Singing, Dancing Success Joe Massara & Olga Stassoff in *Tipsy Topsy Turvy* at the Grand Theatre.

271. EXT. BACK SEAT OF POLICE CAR
The car is moving at a high rate of speed. Flaherty sees something out of scene.

FLAHERTY (excitedly):
There he is. It's Rico all right. Pull up, Ed.

272. EXT. CAR MED. SHOT
Brakes scream as car comes to a sudden stop. Flaherty and others quickly get out.

273. EXT. LONG SHOT
shooting from behind Rico who is foreground of picture. Rico stands near the billboard. Shooting past him, we see the police car and the three detectives, with drawn guns, advancing toward him.

274. EXT. CLOSE-UP FLAHERTY MOVING SHOT
His gun is drawn. He advances toward Rico.

FLAHERTY:
Stick 'em up, boy. And keep 'em up.

275. EXT. CLOSE-UP RICO
An enigmatic grin playing around the corners of his mouth. He shrugs his shoulders, starts to reach toward the inside of his coat.[64]

276. EXT. CLOSE-UP FLAHERTY
He fires three or four shots.

277. EXT CLOSE SHOT RICO
He falls. His hand clutches a comb.

278. EXT. WIDE ANGLE
Flaherty and others run into scene. Rico lies half-sprawled, half-propped up against a corner of the bill-board.

RICO:
Hello, Flaherty—you buzzard. I told you you'd never put no cuffs on me!

FLAHERTY (sees the man is dying):
You should have stuck 'em up when I asked you to.

Rico defiantly grins up at him—feebly tries to get his hand up high enough to comb his hair. A spasm of pain racks his whole body.

279. EXT. CLOSE-UP RICO
He is dying.

RICO (gasps):
Mother of Mercy—is this the end of Rico?

280. EXT. CLOSE-UP OF RICO'S HAND
The nerveless fingers slowly relax their grip on the comb. Rico is dead.[65]

FADE OUT

THE END

Notes to the Screenplay

1 Before the credits the film opens on the front cover of the novel *Little Caesar*. The opening quotation, which survived from Burnett's novel, is changed to the familiar biblical warning: "For all they that take the sword shall perish with the sword." Matthew 26:52.
2 Rico has dialogue: "Get back in there . . . put 'em up!"
3 The rest of the dialogue in scene 3 is not in the film.
4 Scene 6 is not in the film.
5 Joe continues, "Then I'd quit, Rico. I'd go back to dancin' like I used to before I met you."
6 Joe says, "Oh . . . I ain't forgettin' all about the money," and Rico replies, "Yeah, money's all right, but it ain't everything. Yeah, be somebody. Look hard at a bunch of guys and know that they'll do anything that you tell 'em. Have your own way or nothin'. Be somebody."

The end of the scene (after Rico's "Where things break big!") is not in the film, nor are scenes 8–11.
7 At this point Rico says, "There's nothin' soft about me, nothin' yellow. I don't quit." Sam replies, "You got an idea you're good, huh?"
8 Sam's speech ends, "Bat Corilla . . . Killer Pepi . . . Kid Bean . . . and this one here . . . Scabby. What a smart guy he is."
9 An added moment is Rico's acknowledgment—uncertain and then proud—of his nickname: "Yeah . . . sure." His middle name in the preceding line should be corrected to Enrico.
10 In the film the Third Sequence (scenes 16–29) and the Fourth Sequence (scenes 30–38) are reversed, and scenes 16 and 18 are omitted.
11 Arnie adds. "This bird McClure would be pie for him. He'd twist him around his little finger."
12 Scene 29 is not in the film, nor is scene 31, except for the establishing long shot of Joe and Olga on the dance floor.
13 Rico adds, "And if we get in a jam, you'll have to take a chance with the rest of us." The rest of the scene and scenes 53–54 and 56–58 are not in the film.
14 Instead McClure says, "I'm sorry, folks, but we'll have to go somewhere else." A brief encounter between Olga and Joe in the dress-

ing room follows, instead of scenes 61–64. Joe is nervous about his soon-to-be complicity in the robbery.

OLGA: You like my hair this way, Joe?

JOE: Sure.

OLGA: I used to wear it . . . Where're you going?

JOE: Just to get a package of cigarettes.

OLGA: Well, hurry back, darling. It's almost twelve o'clock and I want to be with you for New Year's.

Joe leaves the dressing room and walks nervously through the ballroom where tables are jammed with revelers, noisemakers, and liquor. He continues into the foyer, then draws a curtain to block the foyer from the ballroom. At the cigar counter he asks for Egyptian ovals and looks at a clock on the wall: it is twelve o'clock.

Director Mervyn LeRoy compressed scenes 65–72 into a montage of overlapping shots without dialogue: Rico with a gun, hotel employees' hands in the air, money being pushed into bags, Joe with his hands up, Tony in the car and looking shaky.

15 The woman does not faint, and Rico's shooting of McClure is not motivated by any aggressive gesture on the crime commissioner's part. He is simply gunned down. Scenes 75–76 are not in the film.

16 In a line from Burnett's novel, Rico says, "Open her up, Tony. This ain't no picnic."

17 Olga's next speech follows, without the business of the gun in the drawer and the mirror.

18 Sam omits the emotional display and says, "McClure? You shot McClure? A million guys in this town and you had to pick the crime commissioner. What did I tell you, Rico? Didn't I say to make it clean? Didn't I say no gunplay?" Rico replies to the tirade, "You think I'm gonna let a guy pull a gat on *me?* Any more of these cracks and this is my last job." (The last line is from Burnett's novel.)

19 Sam, who is pacing but not trembling, says to Rico, "What a fine pickle we're in. You and that rod of yours."

20 "Ain't it got license plates on it?" Sam asks. "Yes, but they're phony," Flaherty replies. "It was stolen on the North Side tonight."

21 Scene 92 is not in the film.

22 Instead of "drinkin' wine" Rico says "cheatin' yourself at solitaire."

23 The film skips now to the Eighth Sequence. Tony is pacing in his room and is not hysterical, as in the screenplay. In scene 106 the dialogue from "Where you going, Ma?" to "You was a good boy, Antonio" is omitted.

24 In the film Tony walks down a busy street in daytime.

25 Instead of this speech Otero (who is not drunk in this scene) says, "Listen, kid, I'm tryin' to tell you for your own good. Now you come with me and get your spli—"

26 Instead Tony says, "I'm going to see Father McNeil." The rest of the scene is not in the film.

27 Instead of the Sam-Rico exchange, only Rico has lines: "Well, I guess that's that. We ain't got any time to lose. Come on, Sam, get yourself a car and let's go."

28 An automobile procession is used in the film.

29 Scenes 119, 121, and 124 are not in the film, and only Otero's last line remains from scene 122.

30 The scream and comments that follow are omitted, so that Rico's next line is "Gee, we're movin' slow."

31 Following tbe insert of the program cover, dialogue is substituted for the rest of scene 127:

RICO (examining the cover): Well, that's the goods, all right. That's the fanciest I've ever seen, Sam.

SAM: It sure is.

RICO: Look at those turtle doves down here. "Friendship and loyalty," huh? Well, how do you like that, Sam?

SAM: Pretty good, Rico.

RICO: You know, Otero was telling me I didn't look good in a derby. What do you think?

SAM: Why, it's just like you, Rico.

RICO: Yeah, I thought so too. I guess I'll stick to them from now on. (Reading aloud Sam's testimonial.) "Compliments to a true pal, Mr. C. Bandello, from a true pal, Mr. Sam Vettori." Well, that's nice. I appreciate. That's swell of you. "Remember the river." That's clever.

32 Scenes 130, 132, and 134 are not in the film.

33 The phrase "all you guys gathered together" is instead "all you gents with your molls here." Otherwise, Rico's speech is lifted verbatim from the novel.

34 There is additional dialogue during which Pete Montana moves away from the photographer's camera while Sam preens for it.

PETE: I'll see you later, Rico.

RICO: Aw, don't go away, Pete, will you? We're gonna have our pictures taken.

PETE: I haven't had my picture taken in the last fifteen years.

In place of scene 136 Rico and Sam pose for the camera. When it goes off like a gun, both Rico and Sam jump a little, suddenly vulnerable.

35 Rico's speech beings, "Bad business to quit on me, Sam. One guy tried that on me once."

36 The rest of scene 144 is not in the film, and in scene 145 only Joe's rushing into the telephone booth remains.

37 Scenes 149, 154, and 156 are not in the film.

38 Instead of Pepi's last line he says, "They thought they hit the target, Boss, but bullets just bounce off you." The preceding scene is not in the film.

39 Arnie does not show signs of extreme terror in the film.

40 Rico continues, "And you can take your hats and beat it. The first thing you know you'll be arrested for firing a rod in the city limits. Well, I guess that's about all. Pleasant trip, gents." (To his men.) "Come on, boys."

41 The men group around Sam, who is enjoying the newspaper item. Scabby asks. "Well, boys, what do you think of it?" "Scabby, you're in the wrong racket. It's perfect," replies a gang member. Scene 183 is not in the film.

42 The sequence ends here and the film picks up at scene 198.

43 An amusing moment in the film occurs when Rico greets the butler with a little wave and a bright "Hello" and seems surprised when the butler begins removing the coat. "Huh? Oh, yeah, thanks, thanks very much," says Rico as the butler takes his hat and coat.

44 For "some dump you got" substitute a dialogue sequence:
RICO: Some joint you got here.
BIG BOY: It'll do.
RICO: Yeah, I bet all this trick furniture set you back plenty.
BIG BOY: Well, they don't exactly give it away with cigar coupons.
RICO: I'll tell the world.

45 Scene 200 begins with a title card: "Rico continued to take care of himself, his hair and his gun—with excellent results."

46 To end scene 201 Otero replies, "Sure, Boss, pretty soon you'll be running the whole town." Rico says, "Otero, you said a mouthful." After the butler announces Massara's arrival in the next scene, this dialogue sequence follows:
RICO: I'll see him in a minute.
OTERO: What's Joe want around here? He hasn't been near any of us for months.
RICO: I sent for him. I heard that somebody in Detroit got to Flaherty

and told him to start working on a dancer at the Bronze Peacock if he wanted to find out who shot McClure.

OTERO: Gee, Boss, you're wise to everything before it happens.

RICO: Yeah, I don't miss much. I'll soon find out if Flaherty's been working on Joe after I've had a little talk with him.

At the end of scene 202 Joe refuses the cigar, as well as an offer of a cocktail or brandy.

47 Rico continues, "It gives you a swell front, but it ain't my idea of a man's game."

48 Substitute for Joe: "I ain't gonna spill anything, if that's what you're scared of. You think I want my neck stretched?" Scene 206 is not in the film.

49 They are heard in the film: "Oh, hello, Big Boy. No, I don't want that guy. I don't trust him. Yeah, I got a kid by the name of Joe Massara'll help me." The rest of the scene is omitted.

50 This sequence should have been called Fifteenth Sequence and the one on page 165, Sixteenth Sequence.

51 Scenes 210–11 are not in the film.

52 Flaherty's last line in scene 219 is "Come on, boys, we're going to a party," and here, instead of Flaherty's line, the second detective says, "Formal or informal?" Flaherty says, "I don't know, but we'll find out when we get there."

53 Director LeRoy substituted an anonymous thumb on the doorbell, which turns out to be Rico's.

54 In the film Joe pushes Olga aside and then stands bravely in front of Rico's gun. The preceding scene is omitted.

55 In this scene only Rico's wresting the gun from Otero and running to the window remain.

56 This additional dialogue follows:

OTERO: Aw, you should have plugged Joe.

RICO: Yeah, I should have plugged him and the dame too. If they ain't squealed about McClure yet, they'll sure do it now.

OTERO: Yeah, from now on we're hot.

57 Rico does not swing Otero over his shoulder and run with him. He stays with him briefly after Otero is hit, then flees when he hears a police car screech to a halt nearby.

58 The dialogue that follows (through "The bulls!") is not in the film, and there is no gun battle. The police capture Scabby and Bat off screen without firing a single volley.

59 A revised line for Flaherty: "Nothing but the bracelets, and we haven't got a thing on Rico either. He's next."

60 To conclude the scene in the film, Ma walks back through her fruit store, opens a wall panel, and comes to Rico, hidden in a secret compartment.

61 "If you be a good boy," Ma adds.

62 Scene 251 begins with a title card: "Months passed—Rico's career had been like a skyrocket—starting from the gutter and returning there." Scenes 249, 250, and 253 are not in the film.

63 Scenes 257–58 and 260–69 are not in the film. Instead, Rico calls Flaherty on the telephone and curses him. Flaherty holds Rico on the telephone so the call can be traced.

RICO: This is Rico speaking. *Rico*. R-I-C-O. Rico. Little Caesar, that's who. Yeah, you're a big guy now, ain't you, shootin' your mouth off in the papers. So I ran off when it got hot, huh? You think I can't take it no more? Well, listen, you crummy, flat-footed copper, I'll show you whether I lost my nerve and my brains.

FLAHERTY: Thanks, Rico, old boy, the same to you and many of them. Come on, tell me some more. The sound of your voice does my heart good . . . Say, why didn't you come to Sam's neck-stretching party, Rico? It was a big success.

RICO: Funny guy, ain't you, Flaherty? You ain't got much longer to laugh. I'm coming after you, see? And I'm gonna put one in your dirty hide for every lyin' crack you made about me in the paper, see? I'm gonna show you who's gonna finish up in the gutter. I'll show you.

FLAHERTY: We've missed you, Rico. The town has been nice and quiet. I'm putting on weight.

RICO: All right, all right, big mouth. Only you better get your hat and start running, see, cause you're all through. Call up the papers and tell 'em that, you rotten, dirty, lyin' copper.

Rico slams down the phone, but not before the call is traced. Flaherty gets his gun to head on the trail.

FLAHERTY: They'll have to build him a special noose to get that swelled head of his through. Well, wish me luck.

64 Scenes 274–75 are not in the film. Substitute:

FLAHERTY: You better give up, Rico. You haven't got a chance.

RICO: If you want me you'll have to come and get me.

FLAHERTY: You better be a nice boy, Rico, and come out.

RICO: You heard me. If you want me you'll have to come and get me.

FLAHERTY: I'll be with you in a minute. (To his crony.) Give me that shotgun. (To Rico.) This is your last chance, Rico. Are you coming out or do you want to be carried out?

Instead of firing a few shots (scene 276) Flaherty sweeps the billboard back and forth with a submachine gun.

65 The business with the comb is not in scenes 277 and 279. Scene 280 is instead a long shot of the billboard showing Joe and Olga in *Tipsy Topsy Turvy*.

Production Credits

Directed by	Mervyn LeRoy
Continuity by	Robert N. Lee
Screen version and dialogue by	Francis Edwards Faragoh
Photography by	Tony Gaudio
Edited by	Ray Curtiss
Art Director	Anton Grot
General Music Director	Erno Rapee

Running time: 77 minutes
Released: January 1931

Cast

Caesar Enrico Bandello	Edward G. Robinson
Joe Massara	Douglas Fairbanks, Jr.
Olga Stassoff	Glenda Farrell
Tony Passa	William Collier, Jr.
Big Boy	Sidney Blackmer
Pete Montana	Ralph Ince
Sergeant Flaherty	Thomas Jackson
Sam Vettori	Stanley Fields
Little Arnie Lorch	Maurice Black
Otero	George E. Stone
DeVoss	Armand Kaliz
Ritz Colonna	Nick Bela
Pepi	Noel Madison
Kid Bean	Ben Hendricks, Jr.
Ma Magdalena	Lucille LaVerne

Inventory

The following materials from the Warner library of the Wisconsin Center for Film and Theater Research were used by Peary in preparing *Little Caesar* for the Wisconsin/Warner Bros. Screenplay Series:

Treatment, by Robert N. Lee. No date. Annotated. 75 pages.
Temporary, by Lee. April 30, 1930. 126 pages.
Final, by Francis Edwards Faragoh. July 7, 1930. 128 pages.

DESIGNED BY GARY GORE
COMPOSED BY GRAPHIC COMPOSITION, INC.
ATHENS, GEORGIA
MANUFACTURED BY FAIRFIELD GRAPHICS
FAIRFIELD, PENNSYLVANIA
TEXT AND DISPLAY LINES ARE SET IN PALATINO

Library of Congress Cataloging in Publication Data
Faragoh, Francis Edwards.
Little Caesar.
(Wisconsin/Warner Bros. screenplay series)
"Screenplay by Francis Edwards Faragoh
from the novel by W.R. Burnett."
Bibliography: pp. 27–28.
I. Burnett, William Riley, 1899–
II. Peary, Gerald.
III. Burnett, William Riley, 1899– Little Caesar.
IV. Wisconsin Center for Film and Theater Research.
V. Little Caesar. [Motion picture] VI. Series.
PN1997.L589 791.43'72 80-52291
ISBN 0-299-08450-7
ISBN 0-299-08454-X (pbk.)

WW

WISCONSIN/WARNER BROS SCREENPLAY SERIES

The Wisconsin/Warner Bros. Screenplay Series, a product of the Warner Brothers Film Library of the University of Wisconsin-Madison, offers scholars, students, researchers, and aficionados insights into individual films that have never before been possible.

The Warner library was acquired in 1957 by the United Artists Corporation, which in turn donated it to the Wisconsin Center for Film and Theater Research in 1969. The massive library, housed in the State Historical Society of Wisconsin, contains eight hundred sound feature films, fifteen hundred short subjects, and nineteen thousand still negatives, as well as the legal files, press books, and screenplays of virtually every Warner film produced from 1930 until 1950. This rich treasure trove has made the University of Wisconsin one of the major centers for film research, attracting scholars from around the world. This series of published screenplays represents a creative use of the Warner library, both a boon to scholars and a tribute to United Artists.

Most published film scripts are literal transcriptions of finished films. The Wisconsin/Warner screenplays are primary source documents—the final shooting versions including revisions made during production. As such, they reveal the art of screenwriting as other film transcriptions cannot. Comparing these screenplays with the final films will illuminate the arts of directing and acting, as well as the other arts of the film making process. (Films of the Warner library are available at modest rates from the United Artists nontheatrical rental library, United Artists/16 mm.)

From the eight hundred feature films in the library, the editors of the series selected for publication examples that have received critical recognition for excellence of directing, screenwriting, and acting, films distinctive in genre, in historical relevance, and in adaptation of well-known novels and plays.